Design Concepts of Operating System

DESIGN CONCEPTS OF OPERATING SYSTEM

Dr. Raj Gurang Tiwari
Dr. Ambuj Kumar Agarwal
Dr. Vikas Khullar
Dr. Durgesh Srivastava

NAMYA PRESS.com

Published by

Namya Press

213, Vardhan house, 7/28, Ansari Road, Darya Ganj, Delhi - 110002.

Email: namyapress@gmail.com

Edition	:	**First Published in 2021 (Namya Press)**
Title	:	**Design Concepts of Operating System**
Author	:	**Dr. Raj Gurang Tiwari, Dr. Ambuj Kumar Agarwal, Dr. Vikas Khullar, Dr. Durgesh Srivastava**
ISBN	:	**978-93-91010-07-2**
MRP	:	
Copyright	:	**© Dr. R. G. Tiwari et. al. 2021 All rights reserved**
Printer	:	**Trident Enterprises (Noida), D-204, Sector-10, Noida G.B. Nagar, U.P.**

Preface

Operating systems are a vital program of any computer system and computer science education. This book introduces the design concepts of operating systems. As computer is eventually embedding in every area though Operating Systems is undergoing express transformation. More sophisticated operating system level software's are developing in every arena of day-to-day life.

This book is dedicatedly written for description of operating system concepts from initial to expert level with help of sophisticated and real world examples. Motive to write this book is to explain the operating system concepts from graduation to post graduate levels through understandable descriptions. Hopefully, experts also found healthy discussions in this book.

The book covers Process Management, Processes Scheduling and Inter process communication in latest technologies. This book also covers technological enhancements for leading high speed and efficient process management techniques. Further this book explains the concepts of memory hierarchy, Memory Management, Memory allocation, Paging and segmentation, Virtual memory, etc., by considering detailed architectural designs and algorithms. Core and detailed examples have been used to illustrate both traditional and modern computing memory requirements. As File System Management and IO Managements is also a major arena of Operating systems design, a firm foundation examples based text is presented in this book

Contents

CHAPTER

1

Operating System: Introduction

1.1 Introduction

A modern computer system consist of one or more processor main memory, clocks, terminals, disks n/w interfaces and other input output devices. Writing programs to keep track of all these components and use them efficiently and effectively is extremely difficult job. If a programmer has to be concerned about how data is read or written on the disk, it is unlikely that any program could be written at all. So it is clear that some mechanism had to be designed to shield programmers from complexity of the hardware.

In order to shield programmers from the complexity of the hardware a layer of software is provided on the top of the bare hardware, to manage all parts of the system and present the user with an interface or virtual machine that is easier to understand and program. This layer of software is the operating system.

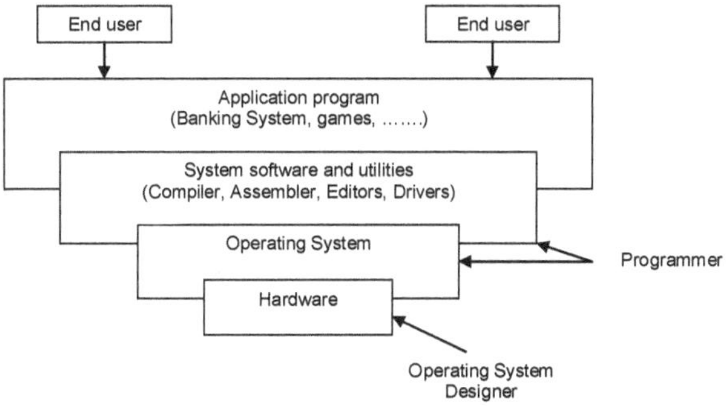

Figure 1.1: Abstract View of System

1.1.1 What is Operating System?

The primary objective of an operating system is to make computer system convenient to use and utilize computer hardware in an efficient manner.

- An Operating System is a system software which may be viewed as an organized collection of software consisting of procedure's for operating a computer and providing an environment for execution of programs.
- It acts as an interface between users and the hardware of a computer system.
- It is a system software that is mainly responsible for Resource Management. It keeps track of the status of each resource and decides who will have a control over computer resources, for how long and when.

1.1.2 Need of OS :

1. User interacts with the computer through operating system in order to accomplish his task since it is his primary interface with a computer.
2. It helps users to understand the inner functions of a computer very closely.
3. Many concepts and techniques found in operating system have general applicability in other applications.

1.1.3 Operating System Services

1. Interprets and executes user command
2. Manages all the system resources (memory, I/O, processor, file)
    - Memory Management
    - I/o Management
    - Processor Management
    - File Management

3. Error detection & response
   - Internal and external hardware errors
     - ✓ Memory error
     - ✓ Device failure
   - Software errors
     - ✓ Arithmetic overflow
     - ✓ Access forbidden
4. Allocates system resources
5. Schedules process
6. Facilitates recovery
7. Performs administrative functions
8. Performs house-keeping task.
   - Collect usage statistics- how many and which kinds of computer resources
   - Monitor performance
   - Used to anticipate future enhancements
   - Used for billing purposes

1.2 Layers and view of Computer System

An operating system conceals the truth about hardware from user. It performs all low-level functions that are required to lead and execute a user's program. Programmers now need not to worry about the details of writing data into the disk, reading information from disk and store them in a memory location.

1.2.1 Hierarchical Operating System Structure

In a strictly hierarchical implementation a given level is allowed to call upon services of lower level, but not on those of higher levels.

What functions should be place in the lowest level (level 1). The one that is used by all resources manager is keeping track of the allocation of resources. This required synchronization of resource allocation. The primitive operations which operate upon a s/w mechanism called semaphore are:

i) P operator (noting that resource is seized or allocated)

ii) V operator (noting that resource has been released)

A semaphore is associated with each resource in the system.

When a resource is requested, the P operator is used to test the corresponding semaphore, if it is off P turns it on and returns. If semaphore is already on the P. P makes a note that requesting process has been placed in wait state waiting for resource associated with that semaphore. Later, V operator issued by another process releases the resource, turns the semaphore on and awakens any process waiting for that resource.

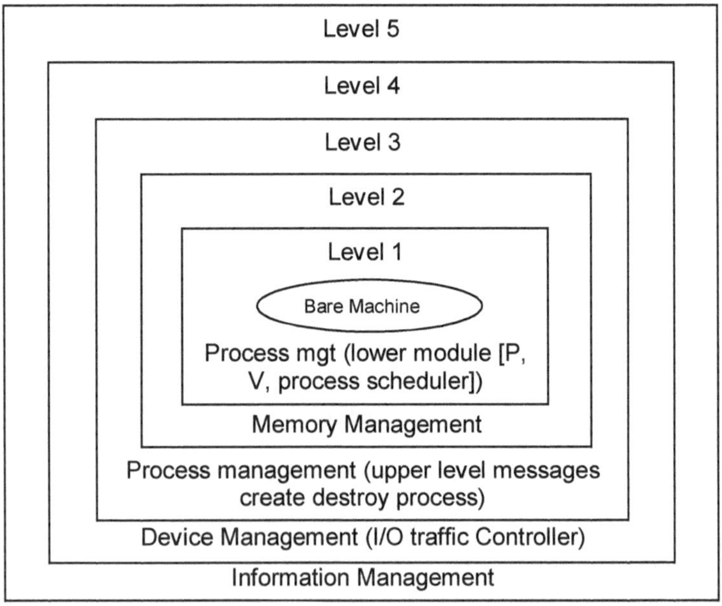

Figure 1.2: Layered view of Operating System

Level 1	**Processor Management lower level**
	i) P Synchronization primitive
	ii) V Synchronization primitive
	iii) Process scheduling (Mechanism of multiprogramming
Level 2	**Memory Management**
	i) Allocate memory
	ii) Release memory
Level 3	**Processor management Upper level**
	i) Create/destroy process
	ii) Send/receive message between process
	iii) Stop process
Level 4	**Device management**
	i) Keep track of all I/O device
	ii) Schedule I/O
	iii) Initiate I/O process
Level 5	**Information management**
	i) Create/destroy file
	ii) Open/close file
	iii) Read/write file

1.3 Interacting With Operating System:

There are many ways one can interact with operating system:

i. By means of Operating System Call in a program

ii. Directly by means of Operating System Commands

- **Command Language**: Most operating systems provide the user with the facility of entering commands directly via an interactive terminal.
- **Job Control Language**: Job Control Languages or JCLs are used to define the requirements and parameters of work submitted to a batch system and would generally be used by computer operations staff in a mainframe environment.

- **Graphical User Interface**: A Graphical User Interface or GUI provides a means of interacting with the system using a windows and mouse driven environment.

1.3.1 System Call

- System calls provide the interface to a running program and the operating system.
- User program receives operating system services through the set of system calls.
- Earlier these calls were available in assembly language instructions but now a days these features are supported through high-level languages like C, Pascal etc., which replaces assembly language for system programming.
- The use of system calls in C or Pascal programs very much resemble pre-defined function or subroutine calls.

User program communicate with the operating system and request services from it by making system call. So the system calls are the direct entry point for lower level operating system services. Corresponding to each system call, there is a library procedure that user program can call. This procedure puts the parameter of system call in a specified place such as machine registers and issues a trap instruction to start the operating system. The purpose of library procedure is to hide the details of the TRAP instruction and make system call look like procedure call. This whole process is known as **kernel call** or **super user call**.

CPU has two modes:

i) **Kernal Mode:** For operating system in which all instructions are allowed

ii) **User Mode:** For user programs in which input/output and certain other instruction are not allowed

1.3.2 Execution of System Call

1) The TRAP instruction switches machine from user mode to kernel mode and transfers the control to operating system.

2) The operating system examines the parameter of call to determine which system call is to be carried out.
3) After that operating system searches the requested system call in dispatch table and find the pointer to service procedure corresponding to system call.
4) Executes the services procedure and return to user mode.

These steps are shown below:

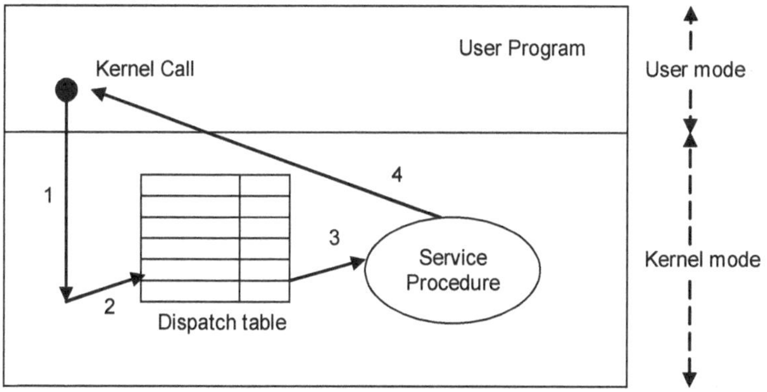

Figure 1.3: Dual mode operations

Transition between user and kernel mode is depicted in following figure:

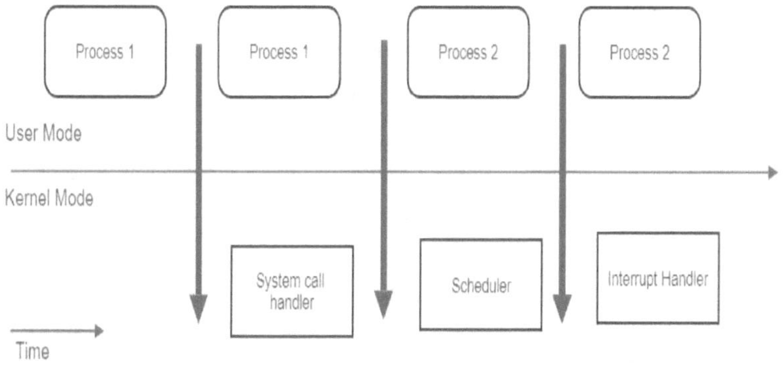

Figure 1.4: Transactions between User and Kernel modes

1.4 System Components of Operating System

The components of an operating system all exist in order to make the different parts of a computer work together. Each component has its pre-defined functions to handle a specific task for operating system. These components include:

✓ Process Manager

✓ Main Memory Manager

✓ File Manager

✓ Secondary Storage Manager

✓ I/O Manager

✓ Networking Manager

✓ Protection System Manager

✓ Command Interpreter

1.4.1 Process Manager

A process is a program in execution. A process needs certain resources, including CPU time, memory, files, and I/O devices, to accomplish its task.

Process Manager performs following activities for an Operating System:

❖ The creation and deletion of both user and system processes

❖ The suspension and resumption of processes.

❖ The provision of mechanisms for process synchronization

❖ The provision of mechanisms for deadlock handling.

1.4.2 Main Memory Manager

Memory is a large array of words or bytes, each with its own address. It is storage of quickly accessible data shared by the CPU and I/O devices. Main memory is a volatile storage device. It loses its contents in the case of system failure or system power off.

Main Memory Manager performs following activities for Operating System:

- Keep track of which parts of memory are currently being used and by whom.
- Decide which processes are to be loaded into memory when memory space becomes available.
- Allocate and de allocates memory space as needed.

1.4.3 File Manager

A file is a collection of related information defined by its creator. Commonly, files represent programs (both source and object forms) and data or any form of audio or video.

File Manager performs following tasks for an Operating System:

- The creation and deletion of files.
- The creation and deletion of directory.
- The support for manipulating files and directories.
- The mapping of files onto disk storage.
- Backup of files on stable (nonvolatile) storage.
- Protection and security of the files.

1.4.4 Secondary Storage Manager

Since main memory (primary storage) is volatile and too small to accommodate all data and programs permanently, the computer system must provide secondary storage to back up main memory. Secondary storage includes CD-ROM, hard disks, pen drives etc.

Secondary Storage Manager performs following tasks for an Operating System:

- Free space management
- Storage allocation
- Disk Scheduling

1.4.5 I/O Manager

The I/O system consists of a buffer-caching system, a general device-driver interface or the drivers for specific hardware devices.

I/O Manager performs following tasks for an Operating System:

- Managing buffer caching system
- To activate a general device driver code
- To run the driver software for specific hardware devices as and when required.

1.4.6 Networking Manager

A distributed system is a collection of processors that do not share memory or a clock. Each processor has its own local memory and clock. The processors in the system are connected through a communication network.

Networking Manager performs following tasks for an Operating System:

- Setup of a networking connection (Wireless & LAN)
- Mechanism for maintaining IP Address (Manual & by using DHCP)
- Managing networking protocol
- Security of network connection
- Firewall management for blocking unauthorized access of computer

1.4.7 Protection System Manager

Protection refers to a mechanism for controlling access by programs, processes, or users to both system and user resources.

Protection System Manager performs following tasks for an Operating System:

- Provides a mechanism for controlling the access of programs, processes, or users to the resources defined by a computer controls.

- Improve reliability by detecting latent errors at the interfaces between component subsystems.
- Early detection of interface errors to prevent healthy subsystem by a subsystem that is malfunctioning.
- Provide a mean of authentication and authorization

1.4.8 Command Interpreter

Command-Interpreter system is a system program, which is the interface between the user and the operating system. This interface can be character based like DOS or it can be Graphical User Interface like Mac and Windows.

Command Interpreter performs following tasks for an Operating System:

- Provides a mechanism to read command from user or process.
- Interpret command into low level language
- Interact with required hardware, resource or file.
- Generate output defined in the command.

1.5 Operating System – Kernel

Kernel is that part of operating system which directly makes interface with hardware system. Its main functions are:

- To provide a mechanism for creation and deletion of processes.
- To provide processor scheduling, memory management and I/O management
- To provide a mechanism for synchronization of processes so that processes synchronize their actions.
- To provide a mechanism for inter-process communication.

As shown in the given figure, the kernel is between system programs and hardware. The kernel supports the file system, processor scheduling, memory management and other operating system functions through system calls.

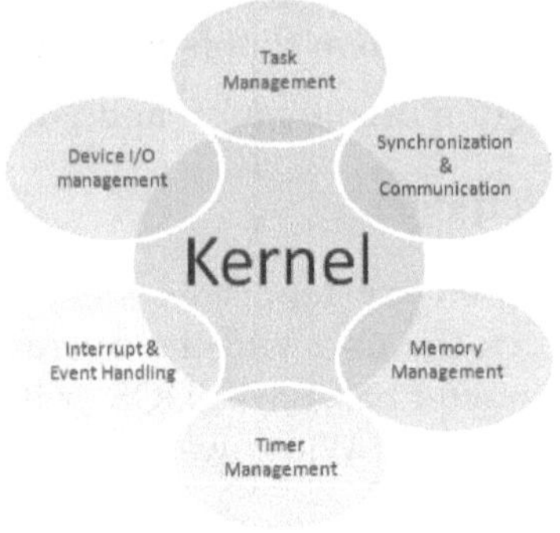

Figure 1.5: Kernel functions

1.5.1 Monolithic Kernel

A monolithic kernel is a single executable handling all kernel functions. Memory is divided into kernel space and user space. And kernel perform functions like scheduling, process management, signaling, device I/O, paging, swapping.

Because many of these functions have low level code, it may appear to be more architecture specific.

Example: UNIX and LINUX operating systems use monolithic kernels.

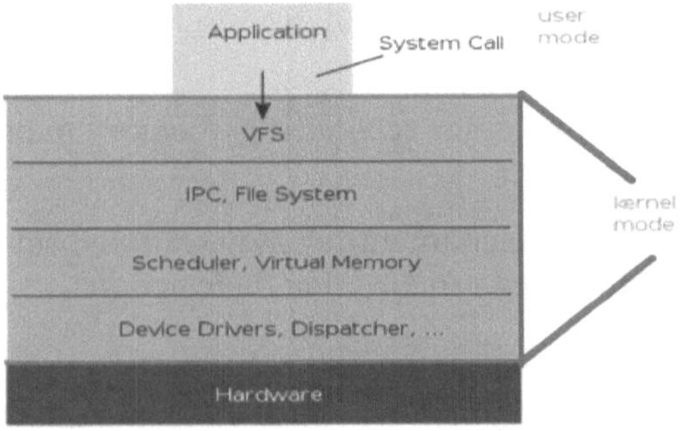

Figure 1.6: Monolithic Kernel based Operating System

Advantages of Monolithic Kernels

- Single executable works fine if you have the memory
- Easy implementation of threading for file I/O
- Very efficient
- Easier to implement

Disadvantages of Monolithic Kernels

- Memory footprint increases in direct proportion to code size
- More complicated monolithic structure requires considerably more time and effort to understand
- Harder to maintain.

1.5.2 Microkernel

In Microkernel architecture most of the OS components runs outside the kernel. These processes communicate by message passing. The Kernel's job is simple; it has to handle message passing and low level process management.

Processed outside the kernel include file system, memory management and I/O drivers.

Since the kernel is very small, and all other processes run outside of it, it may appear more portable.

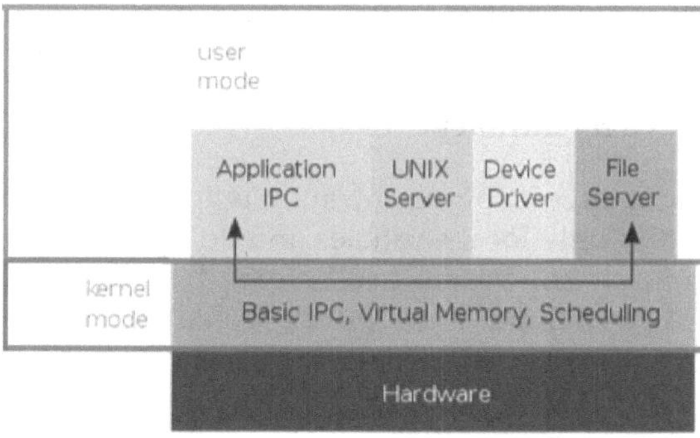

Figure 1.7: Microkernel based Operating System

Advantages of Micro Kernels

- Simpler to understand
- Good distributed structure
- Other "servers" are easily replaced

Disadvantages of Micro Kernels

- 20-25% slower than monolithic
- Complicated message passing infrastructure
- System services creep back into kernel
- More complex exception handling in the kernel

1.5.3 Re- entrant Kernel

A reentrant kernel enables processes to give away the CPU while in kernel mode, not hindering other processes from also entering kernel mode. Thus in re-entrant kernel several processes may be executing in Kernel Mode at the same time.

A typical use is IO wait. The process wants to read a file. It calls a kernel function for this. Inside the kernel function, the disk controller is asked for the data. Getting the data will take some time & the function is blocked during that time. With a reentrant kernel, the scheduler will assign CPU to another process until an interrupt from disk controller indicates that the data is available and the earlier thread can be resumed. This process can still access IO, like user input.

How to achieve re-entrancy?

First way of providing re-entrancy is to write functions so that they modify only local variables and do **not** alter global data structures. Such functions are referred to as "Re-entrant functions". A Kernel that implements "re-entrant routines" are referred to as "Re-entrant Kernels".

Other than using "re-entrant functions", a Kernel can also use "Locking" methods to ensure that only one process can execute a non-re-entrant function at a time.

Difference between Non re-entrant and Re-entrant Kernel

In Non re-entrant kernel mode, every single process acts on its own set of memory locations and thus cannot interfere with the others.

On a "Re-entrant Kernel", when a hardware interrupt occurs, it is able to suspend the current running process, even if the process is in Kernel Mode. This improves the throughput of the device controllers that issue interrupts. What exactly happens is this: When a device issues an interrupt, it waits for the CPU to acknowledge. If the Kernel answers quickly, the device controller will be able to perform other tasks while the CPU handles the interrupt.

1.6 Evolution of Operating Systems

In attempting to understand the key requirements of an operating system and the significance of major features of an OS it is useful to understand how operating system has evolved over the years.

1.6.1 Serial Processing

With the earliest computers, the programmers interacted directly with the computer h/w (there was no operating system)

Programs for the bare machine can be developed by manually translating sequences of instruction into binary code. Instructions and data are then entered into computer by means of console switches, or perhaps through a hexadecimal keyboard. Programs are started by loading the program counter with the address of first instruction. Results of execution are obtained by examining the content of relevant registers and memory locations. I/O devices if any must be controlled by executing the program directly.

In a typical sequence, the editor program is loaded to prepare the source code of user program, next step is to load and execute language translator and to provide it with source code of user program. If the errors are detected, the whole process must be repeated from beginning. After that object code produced from syntactically correct source code is loaded and executed. If run time errors are detected, an assistant program called debugger is loaded.

1.6.2 Batch Processing

The next logical step in the evolution of operating system was to automate the sequencing of operations involved in execution and in mechanical aspect of program development.

The common input devices at that time were card reader and tape drives and common output devices were line printer, tape drives and card punches.

In the batch processing, the user do not have direct access to machine. Rather he submits the job to a computer operator, who batches the jobs together with similar needs sequentially and places the entire batches on an input device for the use by a piece of software known as monitor.

It is the monitor that controls the sequence of events, means as soon as a job completes its execution; it automatically starts loading the next job.

Monitor always resides in main memory and available for execution. This portion is referred as resident monitor.

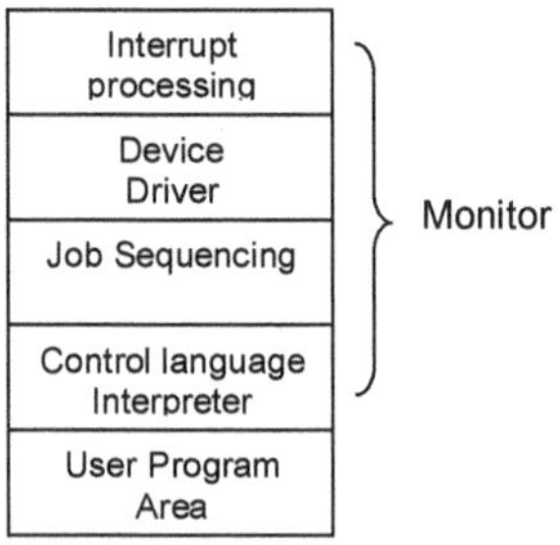

Figure 1.8: Memory Layout in Batch Systems

How Monitor Works

The monitor reads a job one at time from input device, as it is read in, it is placed in user program area and control is passed to this job. When the job is completed it returns control to monitor which immediately reads in next job. The result of each job is printed out for delivery to user.

How a Job Differs from Program

Some instructions are included with user program and data to form a job. These instructions are written in Job Control Language (JCL) which is a special type of language used to provide instructions to monitor. Typical JCL commands include making of job beginning and end, command for loading and execution of program, and command to announce resource needs such as expected execution time, and memory allocation. When a JOB_END command is encountered, the monitor may look for another job which may be identifies by a JOB_START command.

Advantage

i) Reduces the CPU idle time due to slow manual operation.

ii) Offers greater through put than simple serial processing.

Disadvantage

i) As far as program development to concerned batch is not a good improvement over simple serial processing.

ii) Turned around time (measured from submission of job to output received) is quite long.

iii) Programmers are forced to debug their programs off line using post mortem memory dumps as apposed to being able to examine the state of machine immediately upon detection of failure.

iv) Speeds of mechanical Input Output devices are much slower than CPU (an electronic device). This also a major performance bottleneck.

1.6.3 Multiprogrammed Operating System

After batch operating systems, to increase the system throughput and resource utilization a class of operating system that multiplex resources of computer system among multiple active programs were evaluated. They are:

i) **Multitasking:** An instance of program in execution is called a process. A multitasking operating system is distinguished by its ability to support the concurrent execution of two or more active processes. Multitasking is usually implemented by maintaining code and data of several processes in memory simultaneously and by multiplexing processor and Input Output devices among them. As soon as a program being executed encounters any I/O instruction and, it needs wait for I/O to be completed, the processor switch to another job.

ii) **Multiprogramming:** The term multiprogramming denotes an operating system that, in addition to supporting multitasking, provides sophisticated forms of memory protection and enforces concurrency control when process access shared I/O devices and files. Multiprogramming Operating System usually support multiple users.

iii) **Multiuser:** Multiuser operating systems provide facilities for maintenance of individual user environments require user authentication for security and protection and provide per-user resource usage accounting.

Note:

i) In general, multiprogramming implies multitasking but multitasking does not imply multiprogramming.

ii) Multitasking is one of the mechanisms that a multi-programming operating system employs in managing the totality of computer system resources.

iii) Multiprogramming with two programs.

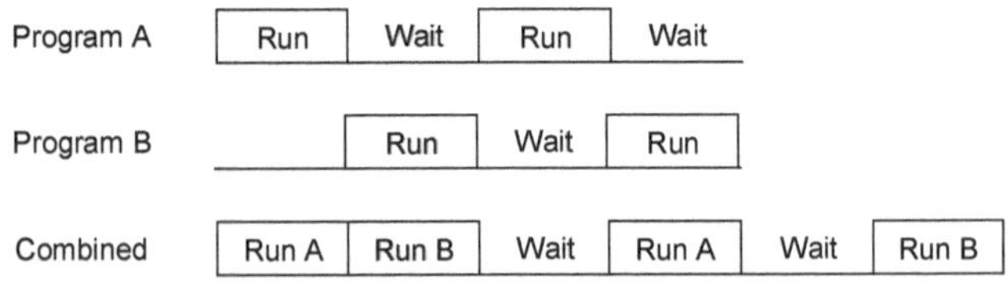

Figure 1.9: Illustration of multiprogrammed execution

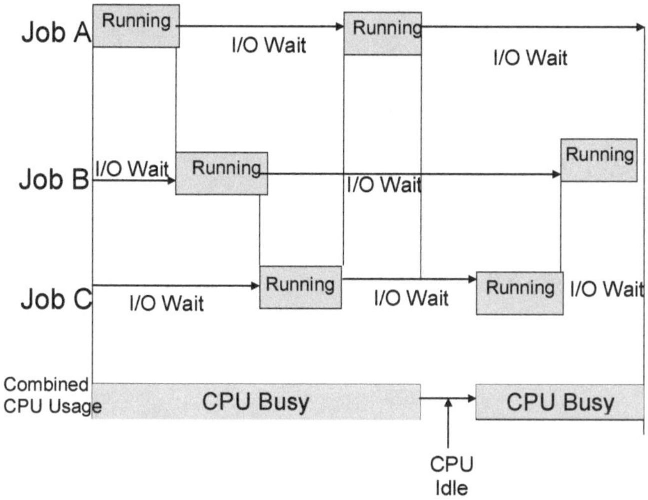

Figure 1.10: CPU utilization in multiprogammed environment

The idea is implemented as follows. The main memory of a system contains more than one program.

The time needed to process n programs is I + CLE _ O, where

I = the sum of the input processing times

CLE = the sum of the compile, load and execute time

O = the sum of the output processing times.

The throughput is n/t = n/(I + CLE +O).

- The fact that the three devices CPU, CR, and LP operate almost independently makes an important improvement possible.
- We get a much more efficient system if the input and output phases overlap in time.
- An even better result is obtained if all three phases overlap.

Throughput of Sequential system :

$$I + O = \sum_{K=1}^{n} (i_k + o_k)$$

With

$$\frac{n}{t} = \frac{n}{I + CLE + O}$$

Throughput of overlapped system :

Let i_k and o_k represent the processing time of input and output of the kth program, and let

$$\mathbf{m_k = MAX(i_{k+1}, o_k) \text{ for } k = 1, \ldots\ldots\ldots, n-1.}$$

Input and output processing for n programs using overlapping can be as low as:

$$M = i_1 + \sum_{K=1}^{n-1} m_k + o_n$$

with a throughput of

$$\frac{\mathbf{n}}{\mathbf{t}} = \frac{\mathbf{n}}{\mathbf{CLE + M}}$$

Illustration :

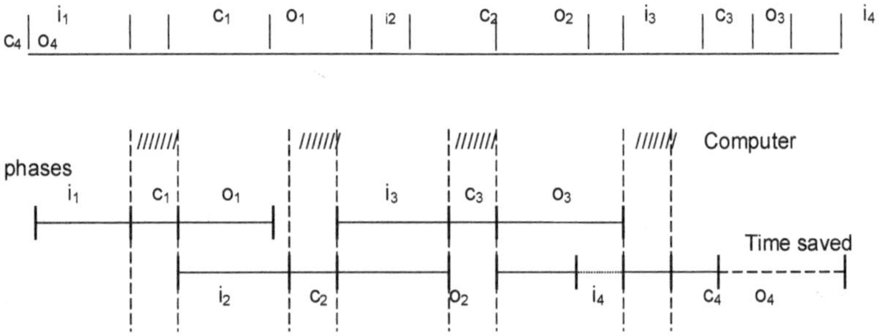

Figure 1.11: Throughput of overlapped system

1.6.4 Time Sharing Operating System

Time sharing operating system is logical extension to multiprogramming. CPU executes multiple jobs by switching among them, but the switches occur so frequently that the users can interact with each program while it is running.

Time sharing OS allows many users to share the computer system simultaneously. Every user program is allocated a small period of CPU time (typically 10 to 20 milliseconds) known as time slice.

As system switches rapidly from one user to another user each user is given impression that the entire computer system is dedicated to him, even though it is being shared among users.

1.6.5 Real Time System

It is special purpose operating system. It is used when rigid time requirements have been placed on the operation of processor or data flow. It is used as control device in a dedicated system.

A real time system has well defined, fixed time constraints. Processing must be done within defined constraints otherwise system will fail. That means a real time system, functions correctly only if it returns the correct result within its time constraints.

Thus real time operating system are used in environments where large number of events, mostly external to computer system, must be accepted and processed in a short time or within certain deadlines. Such applications include industrial control, telephone switching equipment, weather forecasting, flight control etc.

A primary objective of real time system is to provide quick event response time and thus meet the scheduling deadlines. User convenience and resource utilization are of secondary concern to real time system designers.

Difficulty in Writing OS for Real Time System Environment

The main difficulty is keeping the operating system within the fixed time constraints of a real-time system. If the system does not complete a task in a certain time frame, it may cause a breakdown of the entire system it is running. Therefore when writing an operating system for a real-time system, the writer must be sure that his scheduling schemes don't allow response time to exceed the time constraint.

1.6.6 Multiprocessor System

There are basically two ways to increase the speed of computer system:

i) By using high speed components architecturally. Such components tend to be expensive and are often less reliable than standard.

ii) By introducing multiprocessor system which provide an appealing architecture alternative for improving performs of computer systems by coupling a number of low cost standard processors.

Thus multiprocessor system has more than one processor in close communication, sharing the computer bus, clock and sometimes memory and devices.

Multiprocessing can be applied to provide

i) **Increased system throughput** by executing a number of different user process on different processors in parallel.

ii) **Application speedup** by executing some portion of the application in parallel.

   Note:

   - Throughput can be improved by executing a number of unrelated user process on different processes in parallel. Thus throughput is improved by completing large number of tasks in a unit time.
   - Application speedup may be obtained by exploiting parallelism within an application and by creating multiple processes or threads that may be schedule for execution on different processes.

iii) **Economy of Scale:** Multiprocessors systems can save more than single processors systems, because they can share peripherals, mass storage and power supplies.

iv) **Fault Tolerance:** If functions can be distributed properly among several processors, then failure of one processor will not halt the system, but it will be just slow. If we have to process and one fails then remaining nine processors will share the work of failed processor. Thus the entire system will run 10% slower rather than failing altogether.

Note:

The speed up ratio with N processors is not N, rather it is less than N. It is just because when multiple processors cooperate on a task, a certain amount of overhead is incurred in keeping all the parts working correctly. This overhead, plus contention for shared resources lowers the expected gain from additional processors.

Design Issues for Multiprocessor Systems

The most common multiprocessor systems use following policies .

i) **Symmetric Multiprocessing (SMP):** In this, each processor runs an identical copy of operating system, and these copies communicate with another as needed.

ii) **Asymmetric Multiprocessing (AMP):** In this each processor is assigned a specific task. A master processor controls the system. The other processors either look of master for instruction or have predefined task.

1.6.7 Distributed Systems

1) Distributed computer system is a collection of autonomous computer systems capable of communication and cooperation via their hardware and software interconnections. Distributed computer systems are generally characterized by:

   i) Absence of shared memory

   ii) Unpredictable inter node communication delays.

   In other words, distributed system is a collection of loosely coupled processor interconnected by a communication network. These processors are referred to by a number of names such as sites, nodes, computers, machines or hosts depending on the context in which they are mentioned.

2) distributed OS governs the operation of distributed system and provides a virtual machine system abstraction to its user.

Advantage of Distributed System

i) **Transparency:** Component and resource distribution is hidden from the users unless they explicitly demand it.

ii) Resource sharing and load balancing.

iii) Information sharing

iv) Reliability, availability and fault tolerance

v) Communication

In the distributed operating system, the users access remote resources in the same manner as they do local resources. Data and process migration from one site to another is under the control of distributed operating system.

1.6.8 Network Operating System

A network operating system provides an environment in which users who are aware of multiplicity of machines, can access remote resources by either logging into appropriate remote machine or transferring data from remote machine to their own machine.

1.7 Concept of Spooling

Spool stands for simultaneous peripheral operations on line.

Spooling is the use of secondary memory as, buffer storage to reduce processing delays when transferring data between peripheral equipment and the processor.

Spooling was one of the earliest applications of multiprogramming. Jobs are entered via card reader and copied onto disk. Whenever job is finished, operating system could load a new job from disk and starts execution. Printable output generated by running program is written to another disk file, while a printing program constantly prints the data.

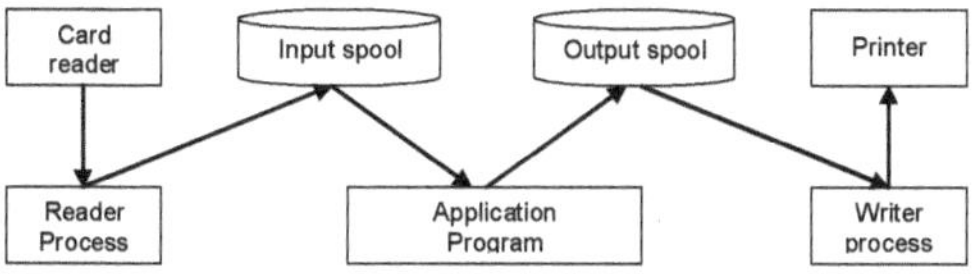

Figure 1.12: Spooling System

1.7.1 Benefits of Spooling

i) Access to slow peripherals is restricted to one program namely spool print program.

ii) Sharing of devices such as printers between several running programs, avoiding the need for these programs to complete possession of printer.

1.8 Operating System As Resource Manager

An operating system is a collection of programs designed to manage system resources, which may be:

i) Memory

ii) Processors

iii) I/O devices

iv) Information (programs and data)

All the resources are valuable and it is the function of OS to see that they are used efficiently and to resolve conflicts arising from competition among various users.

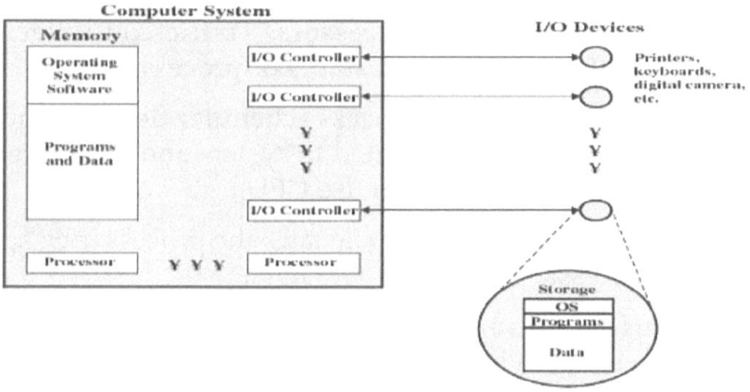

Figure 1.13: Operating system as a resource as a resource manager

Operating system as a resource as a resource manager must do followings:

i) Keep track of all resources

ii) Enforce policy that determine who gets what, when and how much.

iii) Allocates the resources

iv) Reclaim the resources

Thus the main services provided by OS can be grouped as:

1) Memory management functions

2) Processor management functions

3) Device management functions

4) Information management functions

1) Memory Management Functions

i) Keep track of memory what parts are in the use and by whom? What parts are not in use (free)?

ii) If multiprogramming, decide which process gets it and how much

iii) Reclaim memory when process no longer needs it or has been terminated

2) Processor Management Functions: For this OS has following three programs:

i) Traffic Controller Processors: Traffic controller keep track of processors and status of process.

ii) Process Scheduler: Process scheduler decides, chooses from all the jobs submitted to system and decides which one will have chance to use CPU.

iii) Dispatcher: Dispatcher allocates the processor by setting up necessary hardware registers.

iv) Traffic Controller: Traffic controller also reclaims the processor when process relinquishes processor or terminated or exceeds allowed time of usage.

3) Device Management Functions

i) Keep track of devices, channels and control units (I/O traffic controller)

ii) Decide what is an efficient way to allocate a resource (device). Decides whether it is shared or dedicated device. In the case of shared devices, who gets it and how much. This function is also known as I/O scheduling.

iii) Allocate the resource (device) and initiate I/O operation.

iv) Reclaim resource in most cases I/O terminates automatically.

4) Information Management Function

i) Keep track of resource (information), its location, use, status etc. These collective facilities are often called file system.

ii) Decide who gets the use of resources, enforce protection requirement and provide accessing routines.

iii) Allocate the resource (Information) i.e., open a file.

iv) De-allocate a resource i.e., close a file.

1.9 Virtual Machines

Virtual machine can be defined as "A self-contained operating environment that behaves as if it is a separate computer. For example, Java applets run in a Java virtual machine (VM) that has no access to the host operating system. This design has two advantages:

- **System Independence:** A Java application will run the same in any Java VM, regardless of the hardware and software underlying the system.
- **Security:** Because the VM has no contact with the operating system, there is little possibility of a Java program damaging other files or applications.

The second advantage, however, has a downside. Because programs running in a VM are separate from the operating system, they cannot take advantage of special operating system features.

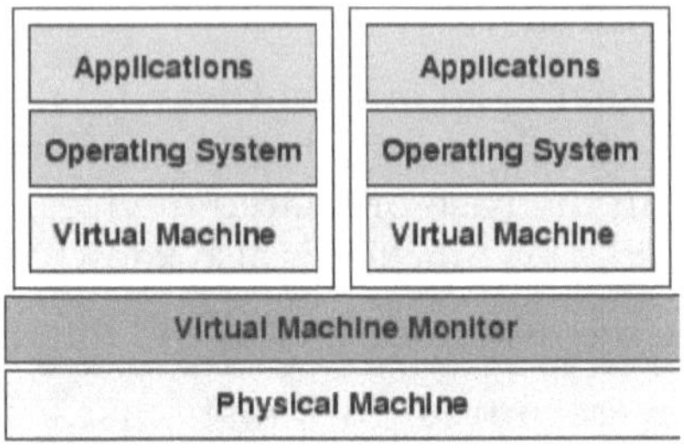

Figure 1.14: Virtual machine

A virtual machine monitor provides a virtual machine abstraction in which standard operating systems and applications may run. Each virtual machine is fully isolated from the rest of the virtual machines.

Above Figure illustrates the traditional organization of a virtual machine system. A software layer called a *virtual machine monitor (VMM)* takes complete control of the machine hardware and creates virtual machines, each of which behaves like a complete physical machine that can run its own operating system (OS). Contrast this with a normal system where a single operating system is in control of the machine.

PRACTICE QUESTIONS

Subjective Questions:

Q1. What is operating system? List the various services provided by operating system.

Q2. Define multiprocessor systems. What are different kinds of multiprocessing?

Q3. "Operation of a time sharing system is identical with operation of a multiprogramming system executing the same program if response time exceeds the CPU burst of every program." Comment.

Q4. The CPU should be in the privileged mode while executing the kernel code and in the user mode (i.e., non-privileged mode) while executing a user program. Explain how this is achieved during operation of an OS.

Q5. Explain following types of operating systems:
- Batch
- Multiuser

Q6. What are the advantages of Multithreading? Discuss diverse Multithreading Models.

Q7. Illustrate the main intricacy that a programmer must conquer in writing an operating system for a real-time environment?

Q8. Whether an operating system is indispensable for computer system? Why

Q9. How does multitasking differ from multiprogramming?

Q10. Briefly explain the roles of each layer in a layered structure of an operating system. Also draw the necessary diagram.

Q11. Differentiate between Monolithic and Microkernel Systems.

Q12. What do you mean by kernel? Explain reentrant kernel.

Q13. Describe essential properties of distributed and Network operating Systems.

Q14. Explain how multiprogramming increases the utilization of CPU.

Q15. Why must a computer start in kernel mode when power is first turned on?

Subjective Questions:

Q1. What is operating system? List the various services provided by operating system.

Q2. Define multiprocessor systems. What are different kinds of multiprocessing?

Q3. "Operation of a time sharing system is identical with operation of a multiprogramming system executing the same program if response time exceeds the CPU burst of every program." Comment.

Q4. The CPU should be in the privileged mode while executing the kernel code and in the user mode (i.e., non-privileged mode) while executing a user program. Explain how this is achieved during operation of an OS.

Q5. Explain following types of operating systems:

- Batch
- Multiuser

Q6. What are the advantages of Multithreading? Discuss diverse Multithreading Models.

Q7. Illustrate the main intricacy that a programmer must conquer in writing an operating system for a real-time environment?

Q8. Whether an operating system is indispensable for computer system? Why

Q9. How does multitasking differ from multiprogramming?

Q10. Briefly explain the roles of each layer in a layered structure of an operating system. Also draw the necessary diagram.

Q11. Differentiate between Monolithic and Microkernel Systems.

Q12. What do you mean by kernel? Explain reentrant kernel.

Q13. Describe essential properties of distributed and Network operating Systems.

Q14. Explain how multiprogramming increases the utilization of CPU.

Q15. Why must a computer start in kernel mode when power is first turned on?

Supplementary Questions:

Q.1. The kernel of a multiprogramming system classifies a program as CPU bound or I/O bound and assigns an appropriate priority to it. What would be the consequence of a wrong classification of programs for throughput and response time in a multiprogramming system? What would be the consequence for the throughput vs. the degree of multiprogramming characteristics?

Q.2. System calls and APIs both enable interaction with an operating system. What are the essential differences between them?

Q.3. How do clustered systems differ from multiprocessor systems? What is required for two machines belonging to a cluster to cooperate to provide a highly available service?

Short Answer Type Questions:

Q.1. What is reliability in the context of multiprocessor system?

Q.2. What is degree of Multiprogramming?

Q.3. How the similar jobs are identified to construct the batch in batch operating system?

Q.4. Define virtual machine.

Q.5. What happens when process completes before quantum in time sharing systems?

Q.6. Define SPOOLING.

Q.7. What are residence monitors?

Q.8. What is meant by Hard Real time systems?

Q.9. Write the role of System Programs?

Q.10. List any two activities performed by operating system in context with memory management.

CHAPTER

2

Concurrent Process and Process Synchronization Process

2.1 Concept of Process

- Process may be appreciated as the program in execution. However many other definitions are also available for this.
- However a program is a passive entity whereas a process is an active entity.
- The key idea about a process is that it is an activity of some kind and consists of pattern of bytes (that the CPU interprets as machine instruction, data, register and stack).
- A single processor may be shared among several processes with some scheduling policy being used by the processor to allocate one process and deal locate another one.

A process is more than the program code, which is sometimes knows as **text section**. It also includes current activity, as represented by value of **program counter** and the contents of processor's register. In addition, a process generally includes process **stack**, which contains temporary data (such as method parameters, return address and local variables) and a **data section**, which contains global variables.

Each process is represented in operating system by Process Control Block (PCB). It contains many pieces of information associated with it as shown in **figure below**:

Pointer	Process State
Process Number	
Program Counter	
CPU Registers	
Memory Limits	
CPU Scheduling Information	
List of Open Files	
———	

Figure 2.1: Process Control Block

2.1.1 Process Implementation

- The operating system groups all information that it needs about a particular process into a data structure called a Process Control Block (PCB).
- It simply serves as the storage for any information for processes.
- When a process is created, the operating system creates a corresponding PCB and when it terminates, its PCB is released to the pool of free memory locations from which new PCBs are drawn.
- A process is eligible to compete for system resources only when it has active PCB associated with it. A PCB is implemented as a record containing many pieces of information associated with a specific process, including:
    1. **Process number:** Each process is identified by its process number, called process ID. (PID)
    2. Priority.
    3. **Process state:** Each process may be in any of these states: new, ready, running, suspended and terminated.

4. **Program counter:** It indicates the address of the next instruction to be executed for this process.
5. **Registers:** They include accumulator, general purpose registers, index registers etc. Whenever a processor switches over from one process to another process, information about current status of the old process is saved in the register along with the program counter so that the process be allowed to continue correctly afterwards.
6. **Accounting information:** It includes actual CPU time used in executing a process.
7. **I/O status information:** It includes outstanding I/O requests, list of open files information about allocation of peripheral devices to processes.
8. **Processor scheduling details:** It includes a priority of a process, address to scheduling queues and any other.

2.1.2 Process State and Transition

The lifetime of a process can be divided into several stages as states, each with certain characteristics that describe the process. It means that as a process starts executing, it goes through one state to another state. The state of a process is defined in part of current activity of that process. Each process may be in one of the following states:

i) **New:** The process has been created.

ii) **Ready:** The process is waiting to be allocated to a processor. All ready processes (kept in queue) keeps waiting for CPU time to be allocated by operating system in order to run. A program called scheduler which is a part of operating system, pick-ups one ready process for execution by passing a control to it. Once the job scheduler decides that process is to be assigned resources, traffic controller is called to create associated process information, and memory management is called to allocate the necessary main storage. At this stage process is in ready state.

iii) Run: When processor becomes free, scheduler program scans the list of ready processes, chooses a process and assigns processor to it. Now the process is called in run state. In the middle of execution it might happen that time slice allotted to this process gets over, then scheduler dispatch program puts this process again in ready state and assigns CPU to another process.

iv) Wait: Some process might require to do disk I/O. Since I/O is slow operation and CPU cannot lie idle till the time I/O is over. Therefore, such processes are put in wait state until their I/O is over. And as they complete their I/O operation they are again put in ready.

When the running process request to access an information (i.e., read a file), information management would call device management to initiate the reading of file. Device management would initiate I/O operation and then call process management to indicate that the process requesting the file is awaiting the completion of I/O operation.

When I/O is completed, the I/O hardware sends a signal to traffic controller in process management, which places the process back into ready state.

v) Complete: When the process completes its computation, it is placed in complete state and all resources are freed.

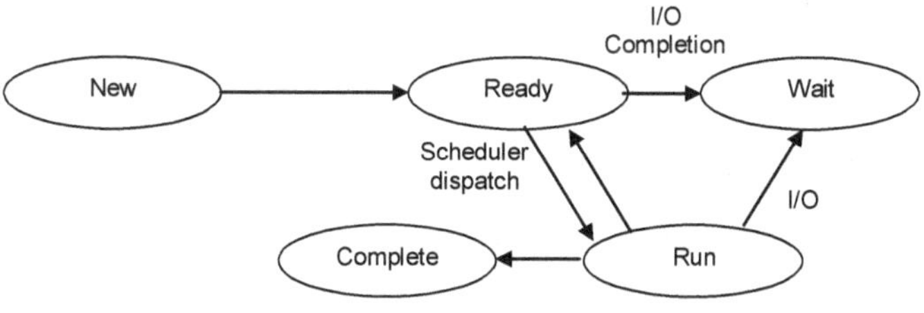

Figure 2.2: Process State Transition Diagram

2.1.3 Context Switching

Switching the CPU to another process requires saving the state of old process and loading the saved state for new process. This task is known as context switching.

This context of process is represented in the PCB of a process (It includes the values of CPU registers, process state and memory management information. When context switch occurs, the Kernel saves the context of old process in its PCB and loads the saved context of new process scheduled to run. Context switching time is totally pure overhead because system does no useful work while switching.

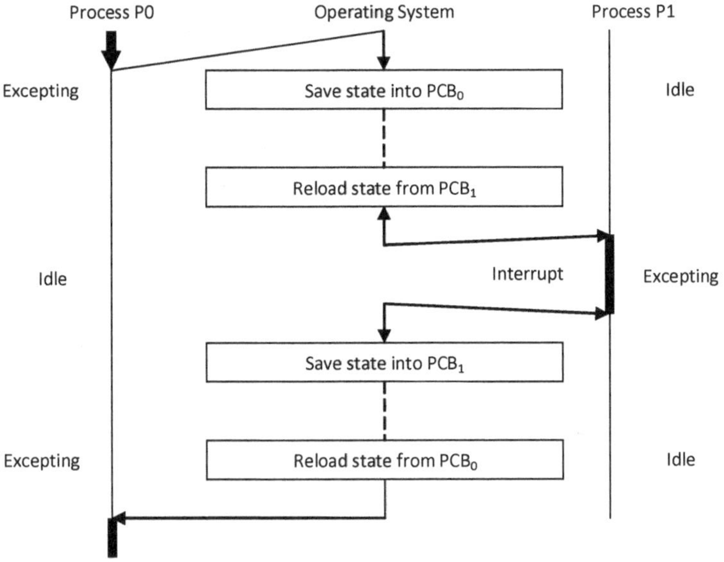

Figure 2.3: Context Switching

2.2 Cooperating Processes

The concurrent processes executing in the operating system may be either independent process or cooperating processes. An *Independent* process cannot affect or be affected by the execution of another process. But a *Cooperating* process can affect or be affected by the execution of another process. Advantages of process cooperation are as follows:

- *Information sharing*

  Since several users may be interested in the same piece of

information, there must be an environment to allow concurrent access to these types of resources.

- *Computation speed-up*

  If a task is broken into subtasks, and each is executed in parallel, the application speedup can be achieved.

- *Modularity*

  The system may be constructed in modular fashion, deviding the system function into separate process or threads.

2.2.1 Issues for Cooperating Processes

- **Race conditions**

  A *race condition* is a situation where the semantics of an operation on shared memory are affected by the arbitrary timing sequence of collaborating processes

- **Critical regions**

  A *critical region* is a portion of a process that accesses shared memory

- **Mutual exclusion**

  Mutual exclusion is a mechanism to enforce that only one process at a time is allowed into a critical region

2.2.2 Cooperating Processes Approach

Any approach to process cooperation requires that

- No two processes may be simultaneously inside their critical regions
- No assumptions may be made about speeds or the number of CPUs
- No process running outside of its critical region may block other processes
- No process should have to wait forever to enter its critical region

2.3 Process Synchronization

A situation, where several processes access and manipulate the same data concurrently, and outcome of execution depends on particular order in which the access takes place, is called **race condition**.

2.3.1 Example of race condition in print spooler

When a process wants to print a file, it enters the file name in a special file named Spooler directory.

A process named Printer daemon periodically checks to see if there are any files to be printed, and if there are, it prints them and remove their names from spooler directory.

The prints daemon also maintains two shared variables.

i) **Out:** Out points next file to be printed.

ii) **In:** In points next free slot in directory.

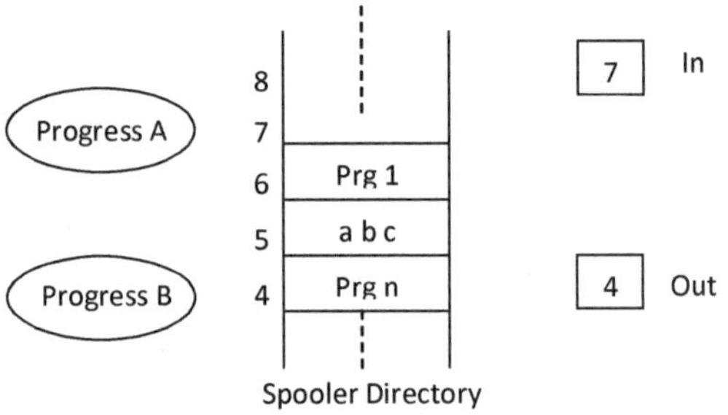

Figure 2.4: Race condition in print spooler

As soon as any process wants to print its file it executes following:

i) Read [in]

ii) Store its value in local variable next_free_slot

iii) Store the name of file in this slot

iv) Increment the next_free_slot

v) Store it in [in].

Consider a situation, two processes A and B decide they want to queue a file in spooler directory for printing. The process A reads [in] and stores 7 in local variable next_free_slot. Just then a clock interrupt occurs and CPU decides process A has run long enough, so it switches to process B. Process B also reads [in] also gets 7 so it stores the file in slot 7 and update it with 8.

Eventually process A runs again, starting from the place it left off. It looks at next_free_slot finds 7 there and writes its file name in slot 7 erasing the name of process B and computes next_free_slot +1 which is 8 and sets it to [in].

Thus B never gets output.

Thus when two or more processes are reading and writing some shared data final result depends on who runs precisely when, such a situation is race condition.

2.3.2 Process Synchronization

To guard against the race condition we need to ensure that only one process at a time can be manipulator the shared thing. To make such a guarantee, synchronization of processes is required.

2.3.3 Critical Section Problem

The part of program where the shared memory, shared file or anything which is shared, is accessed is called critical section.

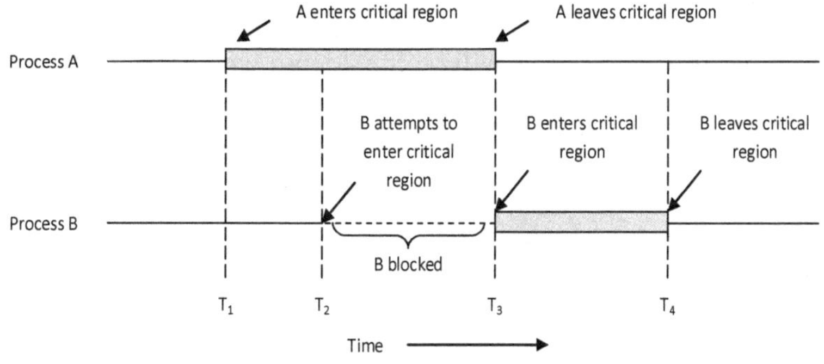

Figure 2.5: Critical Section

Each process has critical section. The important feature of system is that when one process is executing in its critical section, no other process is to be allowed to execute in its critical section. Thus the execution of critical sections by processes is mutually exclusive in time.

The critical section problem is to design a protocol that the process can use to co-operate.

Solution to Critical Section Problem

Each process must be request permission to enter its critical section. The section of code implementing this is the **entry section**. The critical section must be followed by an **exit section**. The remaining code is the **remainder section**.

```
repeat
        | Entry Section |
              Critical Section
        | Exit Section  |
              Remainder Section
forever
```

Figure 2.6: Structure of a Typical Process

Thus solution to critical section problem involves following three requirements:

i) **Mutual Exclusion:** No two processes may be simultaneously inside critical section.

ii) **Progress:** No process running outside its critical section may block other process. Means for entry in the critical section only those processes will be considered who are not running in remainder section.

iii) **Bounded Waiting:** No process should have to wait forever to enter its critical section.

2.4 Proposals for Mutual Exclusion

Mutual exclusion (often abbreviated to "mutex") algorithms are used in concurrent programming to avoid the concurrent use of un-shareable resources by pieces of computer code called critical sections. Most such resources are the fine-grained flags, counters, queues and other data used to communicate between code that runs when an interrupt is being serviced, and code that runs the rest of the time.

On a single processor system the common way to achieve mutual exclusion is to disable interrupts for the smallest possible number of instructions that will prevent corruption of the shared data structure, the so-called "critical region". This prevents interrupt code from running in the critical region. Beside this hardware-supported solution there exist some software solutions that use "busy-wait" to achieve the goal. Examples of these algorithms include **Dekker's algorithm** and **Peterson's algorithm**. In a computer in which several processors share memory, an indivisible test-and-set of a flag is used in a tight loop to wait until the other computer clears the flag. The test-and-set performs both operations without releasing the memory bus to another processor. When the code leaves the critical region, it clears the flag. This is called a "**spinlock**" or "**busy-wait**."

Most classical mutual exclusion methods attempt to reduce latency and busy-waits by using queuing and context switches. Some persons claim that benchmarks indicate that these special algorithms waste more time than they save. Many forms of mutual exclusion have side effects. For example, classic semaphores permit deadlocks, in which one process gets a semaphore, another process gets a second semaphore, and then both wait forever for the other semaphore to be released. Other common side-effects include starvation, in which an essential process does not run enough, priority inversion in which a higher priority task waits for a lower-priority task, and "high latency" in which response to interrupts is not prompt.

The above proposals are discussed in detail below:

General structure :

```
begin
        common variable decl.
        parbegin
                P0;
                P1;
        parend
end.
```

2.4.1 Interrupt Disabling

A process continues running until it invokes an Operating System service or it is interrupted. Therefore to guarantee mutual exclusion, it is sufficient to prevent a process being interrupted. This capability can be provided in the form of primitives defined by the system kernel for disabling and enabling interrupts. A process can enforce mutual exclusion in following way:

```
repeat
    <disable interrupt >
    <critical section>
    <enable interrupt>
    <non critical section>
forever
```

As CPU is only switched from process to process as result of clock or other interrupt, so with the interrupts turned off CPU will not be switched to another process. Thus once a process has disabled interrupts, can examine and updated the shared memory without interference.

Drawbacks

1) It is unwise to give user processes the power to turn off interrupts. Suppose one of them did it, and never turned it on. It would be end of system.
2) The efficiency of execution is noticeably degraded because processor is limited in its ability to interleave program.
3) It does not work in multiprocessor architecture. Disabling interrupts affects only the CPU that executed the disable instruction. The other ones will continue running and can access the shared memory.

2.4.2 Algorithm 1 (Strict Alteration)

First approach is to let the processes share a common integer variable turn initialised to 0(or 1). If turn = i then process Pi is allowed to execute in its CS.

```
Pi :

    repeat
        while turn <> i do skip;
    C.S
        turn := j ;
            Remainder section
    until false
```

In this proposal variable turn, initially 0, keeps track of whose turn is to enter critical section.

Initially process 0 inspect turn, finds it to be 0 and enters its critical section. Process 1 also finds it to be 0 and therefore sits in a tight loop continually testing turn to see when it becomes 1. When process 0 leaves critical section it sets turn to 1, to allow process 1 to enter its critical section.

Drawbacks

1) Continuous testing a variable waiting for some value to appear is called **busy waiting.** It should be avoided because it wastes CPU time.

2) As the processes must strictly alternate in their use of their critical section, thus the pace of execution is detected by slower of two process.

   If P0 uses its critical section once per hour and P1 like to use its critical region 1000 times per hour, P1 is forced to adopt the pace of P0.

3) Most serious problem is that if a process fails either in its critical section or out of it, the other process is permanently blocked.

2.4.3 Algorithm 2:

Problem with Algo.1 is that it fails to remember the state of each process but remembers only which process is allowed to enter its CS.

As a solution :

var flag : array[0..1] of boolean ; (initial. to 0)
If flag[i] is true then Pi is executing in its CS.

Pi : repeat

```
        while flag[j] do skip;
        flag[i] := true;
    CS;
        Flag[i] := false;
    Remanider section ;
  until false
```

Analysis: 1. First checks if other process is in its CS.

2. Else Sets itself and enters CS.

3. When exits CS, resets flag to false, allowing others.

ME is not Ensured:

T0 : P0 enters the while statement and finds flag[1] = false

T1 : P1 enters the while statement and finds flag[0] = false

T2 : P1 sets flag[1] and enters CS.

T3 : P0 sets flag[0] and enters CS.

2.4.4 Algorithm 3:

The Problem with Algorithm 2 is that process Pi made a decision concerning the state of P_j before P_j had the opportunity to change the state of the variable flag[j]. We can try to correct this problem. As in Algorithm 2, we still maintain the array flag. This time, however, the setting of flag[i] = true indicates only that P_i wants to enter the critical section.

```
repeat
        flag[i] := true;
        while flag[j] do skip;
        critical section
        Flag[i] := false;
        remainder section ;
until false
```

- So, in this algorithm, we first set our flag[i] to be true, signaling that we want to enter our critical section.
- Then we check that if the other process also wants to enter its critical section. If so, we wait. Then we enter our critical section.
- When we exit the critical section, we set our flag to be false, allowing the other process (if it is waiting) to enter its critical section.

In this solution, unlike Algorithm 2, the mutual–exclusion requirement is satisfied. Unfortunately, the **progress** requirement is **not met**. To illustrate this problem, consider the following execution sequence.

T_0: P_0 set flag [0] = true.

T_1: P_1 set flag [1] = true.

Now P_0 and P_1 are looping forever in their respective while statements

2.4.5 Algorithm 4 (Peterson's Solution)

It is probably convinced that there is no simple solution to the critical section problem. It appears that every time we fix one bug in a solution, another bug appears.

However, we now (finally) present a correct solution, due to Peterson [1981]. This solution is basically a combination of Algorithm 3 and a slight modification of Algorithm 1.

The processes share two variables in common:

```
var flag : array[0..1] of boolean ;
turn : 0..1;
```

Initially flag[0] = flag[1] = false and the value of turn is immaterial (but either 0 or 1). The structure of process P_i is:

repeat

```
flag[i] := true;
turn := j;
while (flag[j] and turn=j) do skip;
```

```
        critical section
        Flag[i] := false;
        remainder section
    until false;
```

To enter our critical section, we first set our flag[i] to be true, and assert that it is the other process' turn to enter if it wants to (turn = j). If both processes try to enter at the same time, turn will be set to both i and j at roughly the same time. Only one of these assignments will last; the other will occur, but be immediately overwritten. The eventual value of turn decides which of the two processes is allowed to enter its critical section first.

2.4.6 Dekker's Algorithm

Global variables:

turn to indicate whose turn it is to insist on entering its critical section flag [0], flag [1] for the status of each process - true if the process wants to enter its critical section and it is its turn to insist on entering.

```
/* Proces P0: */
flag[0] = true;          //indicate the need to enter critical section
while (flag[1])          //while the other process (P1) is also entering
 if (turn == 1)          // if it is P1's turn
 {
   flag[0] = false;      //reset the flag to false
   while (turn == 1)     //wait while it is still P1's turn
     /* do nothing */ ;
   flag[0] = true;       //indicate entering the critical section
 }
/* critical section */;
turn = 1;                //give the turn to P1
flag [0] = false;        //change status
```

```
/* Proces P1: */
flag[1] = true;          //indicate the need to enter critical section
while (flag[0])          //while the other process (P0) is also entering
 if (turn == 0)          // if it is P0's turn
 {
   flag[1] = false;      //reset the flag to false
   while (turn == 0)     //wait while it is still P0's turn
    /* do nothing */ ;
   flag[1] = true;       //indicate entering the critical section
 }
/* critical section */;
turn = 0;                //give the turn to P0
flag [1] = false;        //change status
```

Petrrson vs dekkers

```
Peterson's: "I want to enter."                    flag[0]=true;
            "You can enter next."                 turn=1;
            "If you want to enter and             while(flag[1]==true&&turn==1){
            it's your turn I'll wait."            }
            Else: Enter CS!                       // CS
            "I don't want to enter any more."     flag[0]=false;

Dekker's:   "I want to enter."                    flag[0]=true;
            "If you want to enter                 while(flag[1]==true){
             and if it's your turn                  if(turn!=0){
             I don't want to enter any more."         flag[0]=false;
            "If it's your turn                        while(turn!=0){
             I'll wait."                              }
            "I want to enter."                        flag[0]=true;
                                                    }
                                                  }
            Enter CS!                             // CS
            "You can enter next."                 turn=1;
            "I don't want to enter any more."     flag[0]=false;
```

The difference seems to be the point where "`You can enter next.`" occurs and the fact that "`if it's your turn I don't want to enter any more.`" occurs in Dekker's.

In Peterson's algorithm, the two processes seem to be dominant. A process seems to force his way in into the critical section unless it's the other one's turn.

Conversely, in Dekker's algorithm, the two processes seem to be submissive and polite. If both processes want to enter the critical section, and it's the other one's turn, the process decides to no longer want to enter.

2.4.7 Bakery Algorithm

This algorithm solves the critical section problem for n processes in software. The basic idea is that of a bakery; customers take numbers, and whoever has the lowest number gets service next. Here, of course, "service" means entry to the critical section.

```
1 var choosing: shared array[0..n-1] of boolean;
2 number: shared array[0..n-1] of integer; ...
3 repeat
4       choosing[i] := true;
5       number[i] := max(number[0],number[1],...,number[n-1]) + 1;
6       choosing[i] := false;
7       for j := 0 to n-1 do begin
8               while choosing[j] do (* nothing *);
9               while number[j] <> 0 and
10                          (number[j], j) < (number[i],i) do
11                          (* nothing *);
12      end;
13      (* critical section *)
14      number[i] := 0;
15      (* remainder section *)
16 forever;.
```

lines 1-2: Here, choosing[i] is true if process i is choosing a number. The number that process i will use to enter the critical section is in number[i]; it is 0 if process i is not trying to enter its critical section.

lines 4-6: These three lines first indicate that the process is choosing a number (line 4), then try to assign a unique number to the process process i (line 5); however, that does not always happen. Afterwards, process i indicates it is done (line 6).

lines 7-12: Now we select which process goes into the critical section. Process i waits until it has the lowest number of all the processes waiting to enter the critical section. If two processes have the same number, the one with the smaller name—the value of the subscript—goes in; the notation "(a,b) < (c,d)" means true if a < c or if both a = c and b < d (lines 9-10). Note that if a process is not trying to enter the critical section, its number is 0. Also, if a process is choosing a number when process i tries to look at it, process i waits until it has done so before looking (line 8).

line 14: Now process i is no longer interested in entering its critical section, so it sets number[i] to 0.

2.4.8 Hardware Solutions (TSL) :

Many machines provide special hardware instructions that allow one to either test and modify the content of a word, or to swap the contents of two words, in one memory cycle (atomically). These special instructions can be used to solve the critical section problem. Let us abstract the main concepts behind these types of instructions by defining the Test-and Set instruction as follows:

The operations of reading the word and storing into it are guaranteed to be indivisible no other processor can access the word until the instruction is finished. The CPU executing the TSL instruction locks the memory bus to prohibit other CPUs from accessing memory until it is done

```
boolean Test-and Set ( Boolean target )
{
   boolean temp;
   temp = target;
   target := true;
   return( target );
}
```

The important characteristic is that these instructions are executed atomically; that is, in one memory cycle. Thus if two Test-and Set instructions are executed simultaneously (each on a different cpu), they will be executed sequentially in some arbitrary order.

If the machine supports the Test-and Set instruction, then mutual exclusion can be implemented by declaring a boolean variable lock, initialized to false.

```
repeat
        while Test-and Set(lock) do skip;
        critical section
        lock := false;
        remainder section
   until false;
```

Drawbacks of Peterson and TSL Approach

1) **Busy-waiting:** When a process is waiting for access to a critical section, it sits in a tight loop and consumes the CPU time.
2) **Starvation:** When a process leaves a critical section and more than one process is waiting, the selection of waiting process is arbitrary. Thus some process could indefinitely be denied access.
3) **Priority Inversion Problem:** Consider a computer with two processes: H with higher priority and L with low priority. The scheduling rules are such that H is run whenever it is in ready state. At a certain moment with L in its critical section, H becomes ready to run (means its Input/Output operation completes), H now begins busy waiting. But since L is never scheduled while H is running, L never gets chance to leave its critical region, so H loops forever. This situation is sometimes known as priority inversion problem.

2.4.9 Sleep and Wakeup

To avoid the busy waiting two other inter-process communication primitives were used:

i) Sleep: It is a system call which causes the caller to block when it is not allowed to enter their critical section.

ii) Wakeup: It is used as wakeup call for a sleeping process.

Whenever a process goes for sleep its state is switched to waiting state. Then control is transferred to CPU scheduler, which selects another process to execute.

Whenever any other process wakes it, its state is again switched to ready state. The process is then placed in ready queue. The CPU may or may not be switched from running process to newly ready process depending on CPU-scheduling algorithm.

2.4.10 Semaphores:

- The solutions to the mutual exclusion problem presented in the last section are not easy to generalize to more complex problems.
- To overcome this difficulty, a new synchronization tool, called a semaphore, was introduced by Dijkstra [1965a].
- A semaphore S is an integer variable that, apart from initialization, can be accessed only through two standard atomic operations: P and V. The classical definitions of P and V are:

P(S): while S <= 0 do skip;
S : = S – 1;

V(S): S: = S + 1;

Modifications to the integer value of the semaphore in the P and V operations are executed indivisibly. That is, when one process modifies the semaphore value, no other process can simultaneously modify that same semaphore value. In addition, in the case of the P(S), the testing of the integer value of S(S d" 0), and its possible modification (S := S – 1) must also be executed without interruption

Usage:

1. Semaphores can be used in dealing with the n-process critical section problem. The n processes share a common

semaphore, mutex, initialized to 1. Each process P_i is organized as follows:

repeat

P(mutex);

critical section

V(mutex);

remainder section

until false;

2. Semaphores as Synchronization Tool:

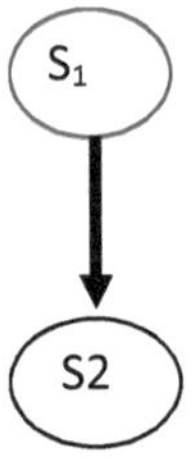

Consider two concurrently running processes: P_1 with a statement S_1, and P_2 with a statement S_2. Suppose that we require that S_2 be executed only after S1 has completed. This scheme can be readily implemented by letting P_1 and P_2 share a common semaphore synch, initialized to 0, and by inserting the statements:

$S_{1;}$

V(synch); in process $P_{1,}$ and the statements

P(synch);

$S_{2;}$

in process $P_{2.}$ Since synch is initialized to 0, P_2 will execute S_2 only after P_1 has invoked V(synch), which is after S_1.

The disadvantage of the semaphore definition given above is that it requires busy-waiting, i.e., while a process is in its critical region, any either process it trying to enter its critical region must continuously loop in the entry code. It's clear that through busy-waiting, CPU cycles are wasted that some other processes might use productively.

Semaphore definition with out busy-waiting:

To overcome busy-waiting, we modify the definition of the wait and signal operations. When a process executes the wait operation and finds that the semaphore value is not positive, the process blocks itself. The block operation places the process into a waiting state. Using a scheduler the CPU then can be allocated to other processes which are ready to run.

A process that is blocked, i.e. waiting on a semaphore S, should be restarted by the execution of a signal operation by some other processes, which changes its state from blocked to ready. To implement a semaphore under this condition, we define a semaphore as a record:

To implement semaphore for avoiding busy-waiting we define a semaphore as a record.

```
struct semaphore
{
        int value;
        process *L;          //List of processes
}
```

Each semaphore has an integer value and a list of processes. When a process must wait on a semaphore, it is added to the list of processes. A V operation removes one process from the list of waiting processes and awakens it.

The semaphore operations can now be defined as:

```
P(S):   S. value := S. value – 1;
        if S. value < 0
         then begin
          add this process to S.L;
          block;
        end;

V(S):   S. value := S. value + 1;
        if S.value d" 0
        then begin
          remove this process P from S.L;
          wakeup(P);
        end;
```

For simplification P and V operations can be written as:

P(s): **if** s.value = 1
then s = 0 /* lower semaphore */
else BLOCK calling process on s
DISPATCH a ready process

V(s): **if** the list of processes waiting on s is nonempty
then WAKE UP a process waiting on s
else s = 1 /* raise semaphore */

Table shows a sequence of 14 states of 6 processes invoking P and V operations on semaphores. Initially, none of the processes is in its critical

Action			**Resulting Status**		
invoking process		operation invoked	running in CS	blocked on s	value of s
1	A	P(s)	A		1
2	A	V(s)			0
3	B	P(s)	B		1
4	C	P(s)	B	C	0
5	D	P(s)	B	C,D	0
6	E	P(s)	B	C,D,E	0
7	B	V(s)	D	C,E	0
8	F	P(s)	D	C,E,F	0
9	D	V(s)		C,F	0
11	none of A,..,F		E	C,F	0
12	E	V(s)	F	C	0
13	F	V(s)	C		0

2.5 Producer and Consumer Problem

Two processes share a common fixed size buffer. One of them, the producer, puts the information into the buffer and another one consumer which takes it out and consumes it. The whole process is described below:

Producer-Consumer Processes:

- For maximizing throughput and better system performance, approaches should be made to allow P-C processes to run concurrently.
- Producer should produce into Buffer and Consumer should consume from buffer.
- A Producer can produce into one buffer while the consumer is consuming from other buffer. P-C must be synchronized so that Consumer does not try to consume items which are not yet been produced.

Unbounded Buffer Producer-Consumer :

- No limit on the number of buffers.
- The consumer may have to wait for new items, but the producer can always produce new items i.e. buffers are of unlimited capacity there are always empty buffers.

Bounded Buffer Producer-Consumer : Assumes that there is a fixed number 'n' of buffer.

Solution to Bounded Buffer Problem :

Data Structure : 1. Circular Array (shared Pool of Buffers)
2. Two Logical Pointers : 'in' and 'out'
in points to the next free buffer.
out points to the first full buffer.
3. integer variable counter initialized to 0.

counter is incremented every time a new full buffer is added to the pool and decremented whenever one is consumed

Typeitem = ...;

Var buffer : array[0..n-1] of item;

In, out : 0..n-1

Nextp, nextc : item;

In := 0, out := 0;

```
Parbegin
   Producer: begin
               repeat
               .....
     produce an item in nextp
               .....
           while counter =n do skip;
     buffer[in] := nextp;
               in := in+1 mod n;
               counter := counter + 1;
           until false;
           end;
   Consumer: begin
               repeat
                  .....
                  while counter = 0 do skip;
                  nextc := buffer[out];
                  out := out+1 mod n;
                  counter := counter - 1;
                  consume the item in nextc;
             until false;
           end;
parend;
```

This implementation may lead to wrong values, if concurrent execution is uncontrolled

e.g. If *counter* value is currently 5, and Producer is executing the statement *counter* := *counter* +1 and Consumer is executing the statement *counter*:= *counter* -1 concurrently, then the value of *counter* may be 4,5 or 6. (correct answer should be 5 because one produced one consumed)

How counter may be incorrect ?

i) counter := counter +1 is implemented in machine language as :

R1 := counter

R1 := R1 +1

Counter := R1

ii) counter := counter -1 is implemented in machine language as :

R2 := counter

R2 := R2-1

Counter := R2

Concurrent execution of statements counter := counter +1 and counter := counter –1 is equivalent to a sequential execution where the lower level statements presented above are interleaved in some arbitrary order. If one such interleaving is :

T0: Producer executes R1 := counter	{R1=5}
T1: Producer executes R1 := R1+1	{R1=6}
T2: Consumer executes R2 := counter	{R2=5}
T3: Consumer executes R2 := R2-1	{R2=4}
T4: Producer executes Counter := R1	{counter=6}
T5: Consumer executes Counter := R2	{counter=4}

⇨ counter = 4 while answer should be 5.

⇨ If T4 and T5 reversed then incorrect counter = 6.

WHY INCORRECT ? Because we allowed processes to manipulate the variable counter concurrently.

REMED : We need to ensure that only one process at a time may be manipulating the variable counter.

This observation leads us to problem of CRITCIAL SECTION (CS) and the part of the program code where process is executing shared variable is known as its Critical Section.

2.5.1 Producer Consumer Problem without busy waiting

When a producer wants to put a new item in the buffer but it is already full, it goes for sleep to be awakened when consumer has removed one or more items.

Similarly, if the consumer wants to remove an item from the buffer and sees that buffer is empty it goes to sleep until the producer puts something in the buffer and wakes it up.

The whole scenario is shown below:

```
#define N100
int count = 0;
void producer( )
{
   int item;
      while (1)
      {
      item = producer_item( );
      if (count == N) sleep( );
      enter_item(item);
      count = count + 1;
      if (count==1) wakeup (consumer);
      }
}
void consumer( )
{
   int item;
      while (1)
      {
      if(count ==0) sleep( );
      item = remove_item( );
      count = count – 1;
      if (count == N – 1) wakeup (producer);
      consumer_item(item);
      }
}
```

Race Condition in Producer Consumer Problem

As the **count** is being used by both processes and access to it is unconstrained, the following situation may occur.

i) The buffer is empty and consumer has just read the count to if it is 0. At this instance scheduler decides to stop running the consumer temporarily and starts running the producer.

ii) The producer enters an item in buffer and notices that **count** is now 1. Reasoning that **count** was just 0 and thus consumer must be sleeping, the producer calls wakeup to wake consumer up.

iii) Unfortunately, consumer is not yet logically sleeping, so wakeup signal is lost.

iv) When consumer next runs it will test the value of **count** already read, finds it to be 0 and goes for sleep.

v) Sooner or later, producer will fill up buffer and will go for sleep. Hence both will sleep for ever.

2.5.2 Producer Consumer Problem Using Semaphores

The producer Consumer problem as discussed earlier can be solved using semaphore as follows:

Data Structure : 1. Circular Array (shared Pool of Buffers with size n)

2. Two Logical Pointers : 'in' and 'out'
in points to the next free buffer.
out points to the first full buffer.

3. integer variable counter initialized to 0.
counter is incremented every time a new full buffer is
added to the pool and decremented whenever one is consumed

Typeitem = ...;
Var buffer : array[0..n-1] of item;
In, out : 0..n-1
nextp, nextc : item;
Full, empty, mutex: Semaphore
In := 0, out := 0;
full=0;empty=n, mutex=1;

Parbegin
Producer: **begin**
repeat
.....
produce an item in *nextp*

```
            .....
            P(empty)
            P(mutex)
            while counter =n do skip;
                    buffer[in] := nextp;
                    in := in+1 mod n;
                    counter := counter + 1;
            until false;
            V(mutex)
            V(full)
        end;

    Consumer: begin
                repeat
                    .....
                    P(full)
                    P(mutex)
                    while counter = 0 do skip;
                    nextc := buffer[out];
                    out := out+1 mod n;
                    counter := counter - 1;
                    V(mutex)
                    V(empty)
                    consume the item in nextc;
                until false;
              end;
parend;
```

This problem demonstrates 2 kinds of semaphore. A two-valued or binary semaphore directly implements mutual exclusion (mutex in the example). Multiple-valued or counting semaphores can implement synchronized counts of shared resources (full and empty in the example).

2.6 Some Classical Problem of Synchronization

1) Dining-Philosopher problem
2) Readers-Writer problem

3) Sleeping barber problem
4) Cigarette Smokers Problem

2.6.1 Dining Philosopher Problem

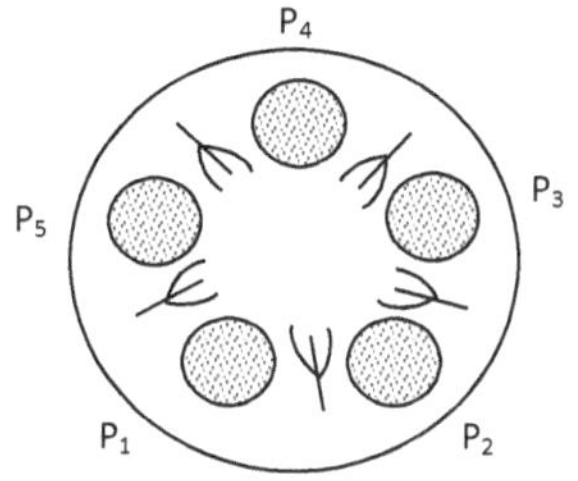

In 1971, Edsger Dijkstra used the example of a group of philosophers to propose a synchronization problem. Five philosophers are sitting around a circular table and each has a plate of spaghetti in front of him with a chopstick at either side (i.e. five philosophers, five plates, and five chopsticks.

Suppose that the life of a philosopher consists of periods of eating and thinking, that each philosopher needs two chopsticks to eat, and that chopsticks are picked up one at a time. After successfully picking up two chopsticks, a philosopher eats for a while and then puts down the chopsticks and thinks.

When a philosopher gets hungry, he tries to acquire his left and right chopstick, one at time in either order. If successful in acquiring two chopsticks, he eats for a while then puts down the chopsticks and continues to think.

The scenario is given below;

```
# define N 5
void philosopher (int i)
{
  while (TRUE)
  {
  think ()
  take_chopstick (i)
  take_chopstick ((i + 1) % N);
  eat ();
  put_chopstick (i);
  put_chopstick ((i+1) % N);
  }
}
```

The problem consists of developing an algorithm to avoid starvation and deadlock. Deadlock might occur if each of the five philosophers has one chopstick and no one can get a second chopstick. The philosopher P_1 waits for the chopstick grabbed by philosopher P_2 who is waiting for the chopstick of philosopher P_3 and so forth, making a circular chain of deadlock. Starvation might also occur independently of deadlock if a philosopher is unable to acquire both chopsticks.

The lack of available chopsticks is an analogy to the locking of scarce resources in real computer programming, a situation known as concurrency. Locking a resource is a common technique to ensure that resource is accessed by only one program or chunk of code at a time. When the resource the program is interested in is already locked by another one, the program waits until it is unlocked. When several resources are involved in locking resources, deadlock might happen, depending on the circumstances. For example, one program needs two files to process. When two such programs lock one file each, both programs wait for the other one to unlock the other file, which will never happen.

A solution of the Dining Philosophers Problem is to use a semaphore to represent a chopstick. A chopstick can be picked up by executing a P operation on the semaphore and released by executing a V operation on the semaphore.

The structure of the chopstick is shown below –

semaphore chopstick [5];

Initially the elements of the chopstick are initialized to 1 as the chopsticks are on the table and not picked up by a philosopher.

The structure of a random philosopher i is given as follows–

```
#define N5
void philosopher (int i)
{
        while (TRUE)
        {
            think ()
            take_chopstick(i)
```

```
            take_chopstick((i + 1) % N);
            eat ();
            put_chopstick(i)
            put_chopstick((i + 1) % N);
        }
    }
```

2.6.2 Readers-Writers Problem

The readers' writers' problem can be defined as follows:

There is a data area shared among a number of processes. The data area could be a file, a block of main memory or even a bank of processor registers. There are a number of processes that only read the data area (readers) and there are also a number of processes that write to the data area (writers). Instances of reader writer problem can be found in online transaction processing system, for example, reservation and banking system.

The correctness conditions that must be satisfied as follows:

i) Any number of readers may simultaneously read the file.

ii) Only one writer at a time may write to the file.

iii) If a writer is writing to the file no reader may read it.

There are several versions of problem depending upon whether readers or writers are given priority.

Readers Have Priority: In the readers' priority case, arriving readers receive priority over waiting writers. A waiting or an arriving writer gains access to the shared data area only when there are no readers in the system. When a writer completes, all the waiting readers have priority over waiting writers.

Reader Process

```
Void reader ( )
{
    while (1)
  {
     if a writer is writing
      then
          { wait }
```

```
            { read }
        if writers are waiting
            then
              wake a writer if no readers are reading
  }
};
```

Writer Process

```
Void write ( )
{
    while (1)
    {
    if (readers reading or a writer writing)
    then
          { wait }
     { write }
     if (readers or writers waiting)
     then
    wake all readers or one writer
  }
};
```

Writers Have Priority: In the writers' priority case, an arriving writer receives priority over waiting readers. A waiting or arriving reader gains access to the shared data area only when there are no writers in the system. When a reader is done with shared data, waiting writers have priority over waiting readers to access.

Limitation: In readers' priority case writers may starve and in writers' priority case readers may starve.

To overcome this problem a weak reader's priority case or a weak writer's priority case can be used. In weak reader's priority case, an arriving reader has priority over waiting writers. However, when a writer departs both waiting readers and waiting writers have equal priority, i.e., a waiting reader or waiting writer is chosen randomly.

2.6.3 Sleeping Barber problem

The sleeping barber problem is a classic inter-process communication and synchronization problem between multiple operating system processes. The problem is analogous to that of keeping a barber working when there are customers, resting when there are none and doing so in an orderly manner. The barber and his customers represent aforementioned processes.

The shop has a barber, a barber chair, and a waiting room with several chairs. When a barber finishes cutting a customer's hair, the barber fetches another customer from the waiting room if there is a customer, or stands by the barber chair and daydreams if the waiting room is empty. A customer who needs a haircut enters the waiting room. If the waiting room is full, the customer comes back later. If the barber is busy but there is a waiting room chair available, the customer takes a seat. If the waiting room is empty and the barber is daydreaming, the customer sits in the barber chair and wakes the barber up.

Figure 2.7: Sleeping barber problem Scenario

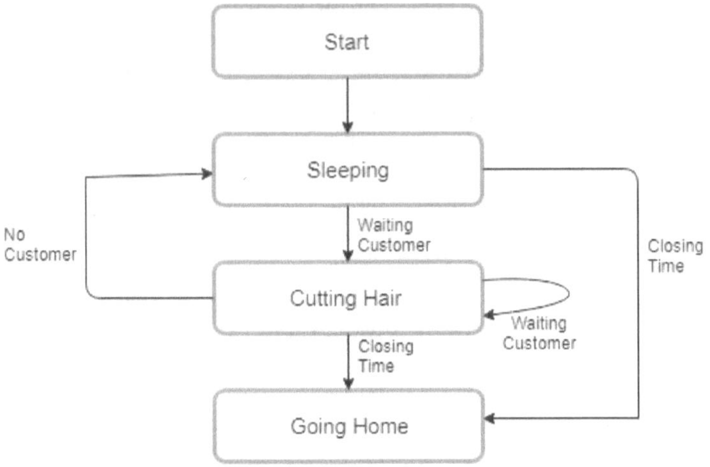

Figure 2.8: Flow of sleeping barber

The problem approximates a situation where several processes queue to get served by another process. The problem arises with attempting to coordinate this activity without bringing about any race conditions.

Solution:

Our solution uses three semaphores, customers, which counts waiting customers (excluding the customer in the barber chair, who is not waiting), barbers, the number of barbers (0 or 1) who are idle, waiting for customers, and mutex, which is used for mutual exclusion. We also need a variable, waiting, which also counts the waiting customers. The reason for having waiting is that there is no way to read the current value of a semaphore. In this solution, a customer entering the shop has to count the number of waiting customers. If it is less than the number of chairs, he stays; otherwise, he leaves..

When the barber shows up for work in the morning, he executes the procedure barber, causing him to block on the semaphore customers because it is initially 0. The barber then goes to sleep, as shown in [Figure 2.8]. He stays asleep until the first customer shows up.

When a customer arrives, he executes customer, starting by acquiring mutex to enter a critical region. If another customer enters shortly thereafter, the second one will no be able to do anything until the first one has released mutex. The customer then checks to see if the number of waiting customers is less than the number of chairs. If not, he releases mutex and leaves without a haircut.

If there is an available chair, the customer increments the integer variable, waiting. Then he does an Up on the semaphore customers, thus waking up the barber. At this point, the customer and the barber are both awake. When the customer releases mutex, the barber grabs it, does some housekeeping, and begins the haircut.

When the haircut is over, the customer exits the procedure and leaves the shop. Unlike our earlier examples, there is no loop for the customer because each one gets only one haircut. The barber loops, however, to try to get the next customer. If one is present, a haircut is given. If not, the barber goes to sleep.

As an aside, it is worth pointing out that although the readers and writers and sleeping barber problems do not involve data transfer, they still belong to the area of IPC because they involve synchronization between multiple processes.

```
#define CHAIRS 5                /* # chairs for waiting customers */
typedef int semaphore;          /* use your imagination */
semaphore customers = 0;        /* # of customers waiting for service */
semaphore barbers = 0;          /* # of barbers waiting for customers */
semaphore mutex = 1;            /* for mutual exclusion */
int waiting = 0;                /* customer are waiting (not being cut) */
void barber(void)
{
    while (TRUE)
    {
    P(&customers);              /* go to sleep if # of customers is 0 */
    P(&mutex);                  /* acquire access to "waiting' */
    waiting = waiting - 1;      /* decrement count of waiting customers */
    V(&barbers);                /* one barber is now ready to cut hair */
    V(&mutex);                  /* release 'waiting' */
    cut_hair();                 /* cut hair (outside critical region */
```

```
    }
}

void customer(void)
{
    down(&mutex);                /* enter critical region */
    if (waiting < CHAIRS)
    {                            /* if there are no free chairs, leave */
        waiting = waiting + 1;   /* increment count of waiting customers */
        V(&customers);           /* wake up barber if necessary */
        V(&mutex);               /* release access to 'waiting' */
        V(&barbers);             /* go to sleep if # of free barbers is 0 */
        get_haircut();           /* be seated and be served */
    }
    else
    {
        V(&mutex);               /* shop is full; do not wait */
    }
}
```

2.6.4 Cigarette Smokers Problem

Assume a cigarette requires three ingredients to smoke:

i) Tobacco

ii) Paper

iii) Match

Assume there are also three chain smokers around a table, each of whom has an infinite supply of *one* of the three ingredients — one smoker has an infinite supply of tobacco, another has an infinite supply of paper, and the third has an infinite supply of matches.

Assume there is also a non-smoking arbiter. The arbiter enables the smokers to make their cigarettes by selecting two of the smokers at random, taking one item out of each of their supplies, and placing the items on the table. He then notifies the third smoker that he has done this. The third smoker removes the two items from the table and uses them (along with his own supply) to make a cigarette, which he smokes for a while. Meanwhile, the arbiter, seeing the table empty, again chooses two smokers at random and places their items on the table. This process continues forever.

The smokers do not hoard items from the table; a smoker only begins to roll a new cigarette once he is finished smoking the last one. If the arbiter places tobacco and paper on the table while the match man is smoking, the tobacco and paper will remain untouched on the table until the match man is finished with his cigarette and collects them.

The problem is to simulate all four roles as software programs, using only a certain set of synchronization primitives.

Solution

Cigarette smokers problem becomes solvable using binary semaphores, or mutexes. Let us define an array of binary semaphores *A*, one for each smoker; and a binary semaphore for the table, *T*. Initialize the smokers' semaphores to zero and the table's semaphore to 1. Then the arbiter's code is

```
while true {
   P(T);
   choose smokers i and j nondeterministically, making the third smoker k
   V(A[k]);
}
```

and the code for smoker *i* is

```
while true {
   P(A[i]);
   make a cigarette
   V(T);
   smoke the cigarette
}
```

PRACTICE QUESTIONS

Subjective Questions:

Q.1. Describe the three state process model. What are the valid transitions of the three states? Also describe an event that might cause such transitions.

Q.2. Show how the following code does not satisfy the requirements of a mechanism to control access to a critical section.

```
shared boolean wantIn [2] = false;
int myPid = 0; // For process 0. Set to 1 for process 1.
int otherPid = 1 – myPid;

wantIn [myPid] = true;
while (wantIn [otherPid])
DoNothing() ;

// Critical Section

wantIn [myPid] = false;
```

Q.3. What do you mean by semaphore? How can semaphore be used to enforce mutual exclusion?

Q.4. How, Peterson's algorithm resolves mutual exclusion, progress and bounded waiting requirements.

Q.5. Define Mutual Exclusion and its need. One solution to the critical section problem or mutual exclusion implementation is with TestAndSet instruction (Test and lock).Explain this approach in detail.

Q.6. Briefly explain the importance of Inter-process Communication in an operating system. Also explain the fundamental models of IPC.

Q.7. The readers and writers problem can be formulated in several ways with regard to which category of process can be started when. Carefully describe three different variations of the problem, each one favouring (or not favouring) some category of process. For each variation, specify what happens when a reader or writer becomes ready to access the database and what happens when a process is finished using the database.

Q.8. Mutual Exclusion primitives can be implemented with busy waiting or with blocking. Discuss the applicability and relative merits of each approach.

Q.9. How concurrency problem are solved with producer and consumer problem? Illustrate.

Q.10. Explain Process Control Block (PCB). Discuss each component of PCB.

Q.11. Explain how a Bakery algorithm satisfies all the three conditions of critical problem solution?

Q.12. Interrupt disabling and enabling is a common approach to implementing mutual exclusion, what are its advantages and disadvantages?

Q.13. What is critical section problem? Is turn passing a proper solution to critical section problem? Give your opinion.

Q.14. Explain the role of interrupts in context switching with the help of proper diagram.

Q.15. Demonstrate that monitors and semaphores are equivalent in so far as they can be used to implement the same types of synchronization problems.

Supplementary Questions

Q.1. Consider the interprocess-communication scheme where mailboxes are used.

- **a.** Suppose a process P wants to wait for two messages, one from mailbox A and one from mailbox B. What sequence of send and receive should it execute?
- **b.** What sequence of send and receive should P execute if P wants to wait for one message from mailbox A or from mailbox B (or from both)?

Short Answer Type Questions:

1) What are privileged instructions?

2) On occurrence of which event, process switches to wait state?

3) Enlist the benefits of OS co-operating processes.

4) What is Daemon?

5) What is a thread?

6) Define Throughput and Turnaround time.

7) Define race condition.

8) What are Bernstein's conditions for concurrency?

9) What are the three conditions that must be satisfies by any solution to critical section problem

10) What do you mean by Priority Inversion Problem?

CHAPTER

3

CPU Scheduling & Deadlock

3.1 CPU Scheduling

CPU scheduling is the basis of multiprogrammed Operating System. By switching the CPU among processes, Operating System can make the computer more productive.

Scheduling refers to a set of policies and mechanisms built into the operating system that govern the order in which work is to be done by a computer system.

When more than one process is runnable, the Operating System must decide which one to run first. The part of Operating System concerned with this decision is called **Scheduler** and the algorithm it uses is called **scheduling algorithm**.

3.1.1 Detailed Study of Process Transition

Queuing Discipline for Process

Whenever a new process is created and submitted to system, it is placed in ready queue. When it is time for OS to choose another process to run, it selects one from ready queue by using any scheduling algorithm. When a running process is removed from execution, it is either terminated or placed in ready queue or waiting queue, depending on circumstances. Finally when an event occurs, all processes in waiting queue that are waiting on that event are moved to ready queue.

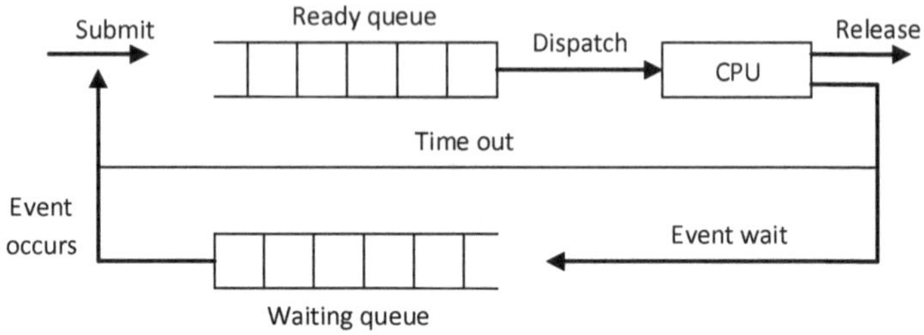

Figure 3.1 : Queuing Discipline for Process

Suspended Process

Consider the case where processor is too faster than the I/O activities. So there may be a situation that all the processes residing in memory have been made into wait state and processor is sitting idle. Thus, even with multiprogramming a processor could be idle most of the time.

If to overcome the above problem memory is expanded, the cost factor matters. Another solution is swapping which involves moving part or all of a process from main memory to disk. When none of process in main memory is in ready state, the Operating System swaps one of the waiting process out onto disk into a suspended queue. This is a queue of existing processes that have been temporarily kicked out of main memory or suspended.

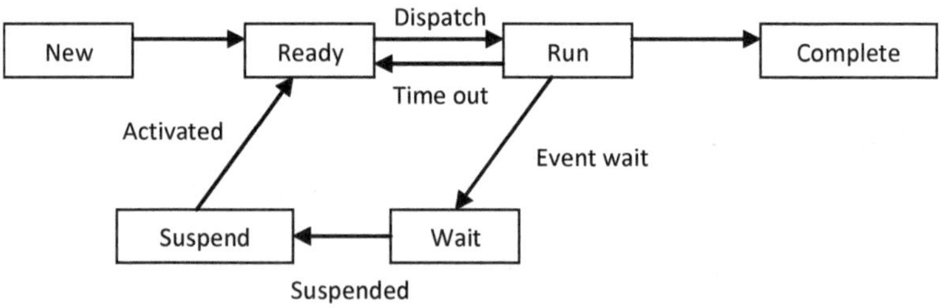

Figure 3.2: State Transition with One Suspend

The space that is freed in main memory can be used to bring in another process. After the swapping out operation, Operating System has two policies for selecting a process to bring into main memory.

i) Can admit newly created process

ii) Can bring a previously suspended process.

But if a suspended process is brought again in main memory of which waiting event has not occurred, means till now it is in wait state (not ready for execution), system load is enhanced.

So before bringing a suspended process again in main memory, it must be determined that process has completed its I/O and now ready for execution. To accomplish this, suspended state is more refined as shown below:

i) **Ready:** Process is in main memory and available for execution.

ii) **Wait:** Process is in main memory and waiting for an event.

iii) **Waiting Suspended:** Process is in secondary memory but is awaiting an event.

iv) **Ready Suspended:** Process is in secondary memory but is available for execution as it is loaded into main memory.

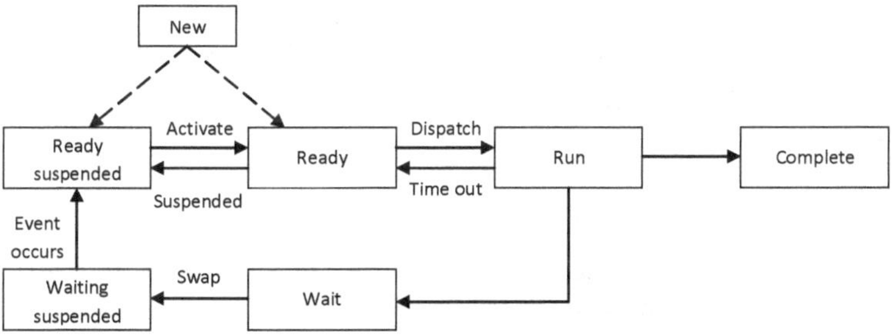

Figure 3.3 :Process transition considering suspended state

Reasons for transition of state are given below:

i) **Wait → Waiting Suspended:** If there are no Ready processes, then at least one waiting process is swapped out to make room for another process. This transition can be made even if there are ready processes available, when Operating System determines that currently running process or a ready process that it would like to dispatch requires more main memory.

ii) **Waiting Suspended → Ready Suspended:** A process in the waiting suspended state is moved to ready suspended state when the event for which it has been waiting occurs.

iii) **Ready Suspended → Ready:** When there are no ready processes in main memory, operating system will need to bring one in, to continue execution.

iv) **Ready Ready Suspended:** Normally a waiting process is suspended but in some cases a ready process is moved to ready suspended state if that is only way to free up a sufficiently large block of main memory. In this case operating system always choose a lower priority ready process.

Note: Newly created process may be admitted in read or ready suspended state depending on priority.

3.1.2 Types of Scheduling

Scheduling affects the performance of system because it determines which process will wait and which will progress.

In general there are three different types of schedulers, which may coexist in a complex operating system.

i) Long-term scheduler

ii) Medium-term scheduler

iii) Short-term scheduler

The following figure relates the scheduling functions to process state transition diagram.

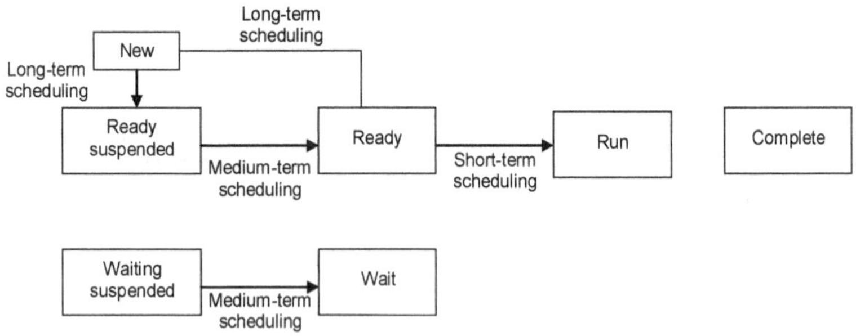

Figure 3.4: Types of Scheduling

Fundamentally, scheduling is a matter of managing queues to minimize queuing delay and to optimize performance in queuing environment.

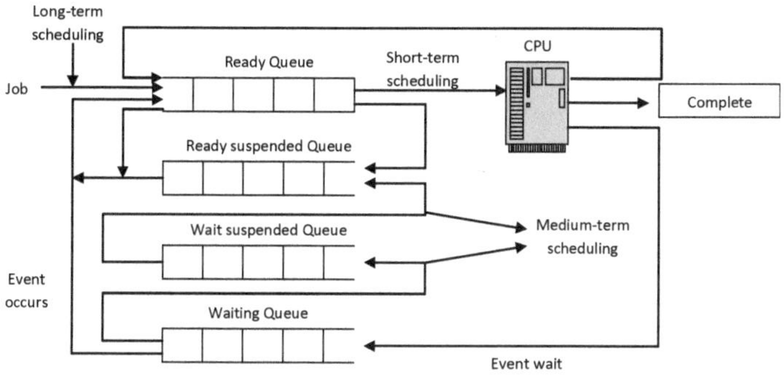

Figure 3.5: Queues in different types of scheduling

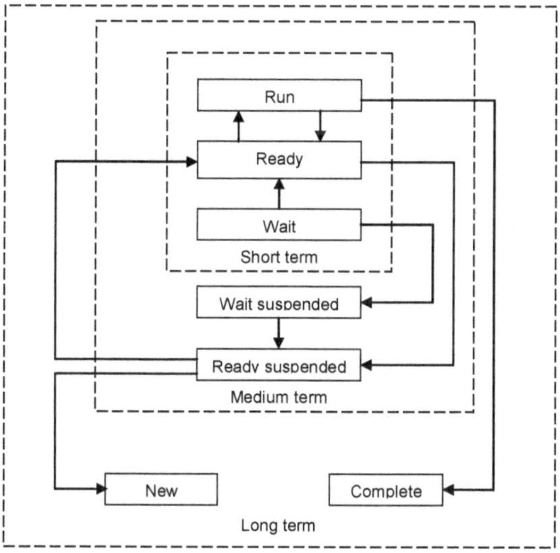

Figure 3.6: Levels of Scheduling

Long Term Scheduler

The long term scheduler determines which programs are admitted to the system for processing. Thus it controls the degree of multiprogramming.

Long term scheduler acts as a first-level throttle in keeping resource utilization at the desired level. For example, when processor utilization is low, the scheduler may admit more jobs to increase the number of processes in ready queue. Conversely, when utilization factor becomes high as reflected in the response time, the long term scheduler may opt to reduce the rate of job admission accordingly.

a) This determines which job shall be admitted for immediate processing.

b) There are always more processes than it can be executed by CPU operating System. These processes are kept in large storage devices like disk for later processing. The long term scheduler selects processes from this pool and loads them into memory.

c) The long term scheduler executes less frequently.

d) If the average rate of number of processes arriving in memory is equal to that of departing the system then the long- term scheduler may need to be invoked only when a process departs the system. Because of longer time taken by CPU during execution, the long term scheduler can afford to take more time to decide which process should be selected for execution.

e) It may also be very important that long term scheduler should take a careful selection of processes i.e. processes should be combination of CPU and I/O bound types.

Generally, most processes can be put into any of two categories: **CPU bound or I/O bound**

- If all processes are I/O bound, the ready queue will always be empty and the short term scheduler will have nothing to do.

- If all processes are CPU bound, no process will be waiting for I/O operation and again the system will be unbalanced. Therefore, the long term scheduler provides good performance by selecting combination of CPU bound and I/O bound process.

Medium Term Scheduler

Medium term scheduler is the part of operating system that performs the swapping function. It:

a) Most of the processes require some I/O operation. In that case, it may become suspended for I/O operation after running a while. It is beneficial to remove these processes (suspended) from main memory to hard disk to make room for other processes. At some later time these process can be reloaded into memory and continued where from it was left earlier. This is said to be Context Switching. The process is swapped in and swapped out by the medium term scheduler. (Context Switching)

b) The medium term scheduler has nothing to do with the suspended processes. But the moment the suspending condition is fulfilled, the medium term scheduler get activated to allocate the memory and swap in the process and make it ready for commenting CPU resources.

c) In order to work properly, the medium term scheduler must be provided with information about the memory requirement of swapped out processes which is usually recorded at the time of swapping and stored in the related process control block.

d) In term of the process state transition diagram the medium term scheduler controls suspended to ready transition of swapped processes.

Short Term Scheduler

Short term scheduler is also known as dispatcher. It determines which ready process should be executed next.

It is invoked whenever an event occurs that may lead to the interruption of current process or that may provide an opportunity to preempt the currently running process in favor of another. Examples of such event may be:

i) Clock interrupt

ii) I/O interrupt

iii) Operating System Call

iv) Signals

The functions of dispatcher are:

i) Switching context

ii) Switching to user mode

iii) Jumping to proper location in user program to restart program.

The time it takes for a dispatcher to stop one process and start another running is known as **dispatch latency**.

3.1.3 Scheduling Criteria

Main objective of short term scheduling is to allocate processor time in such a way as to optimize one or more aspect of system behavior. Generally a set of criteria is established against which various scheduling policies may be evaluated. These criteria are as follows:

1) **User oriented - performance criteria**

   i) **Response Time:** Time from submission of request until first response is produced. The smaller the better.

   ii) **Turnaround time:** This is the interval of time between the submission of process and its completion.

   Turnaround time = execution time + waiting time

2) **System oriented – performance criteria**

   i) **Throughput:** It is the number of processes completed per unit time. The larger the better.

   ii) **CPU Utilization:** That is the percentage of time that CPU is busy. This is the measure of how much work is being performed.

   iii) **Fairness:** No process should suffer starvation each process should get fair share of CPU.

   iv) **Enforcing priorities:** When a process is assigned priorities, the scheduling policy should favor higher priority process.

v) **Waiting time:** It is the sum of periods spent waiting in ready queue.

3.2 Categories of Short Term Scheduling

Short term process scheduling is also known as CPU scheduling. CPU scheduling deals with the problem of deciding which of the process in ready queue is to be allocated the CPU.

The two main scheduling schemes are:

i) **Non pre-emptive:** Under the non pre-emptive scheduling, once the CPU has been allocated to process, the process keeps the CPU until it releases the CPU, either by terminating or by switching to wait state.

ii) **Pre-emptive:** Under the pre-emptive scheduling, process may be interrupted and moved to ready state by OS.

3.2.1 First Come First Served" Scheduling (FCFS)

It is the simplest scheduling discipline. With this scheme, the process that requests the CPU first, is allocated the CPU first.

If the processes P1, P2, P3, arrive in following order,

Process	Arrival Time	Run time
P1	10:00	2 hours
P2	10:10	1 hour
P3	10:25	0.25 hour

Then Average turnaround time may be computed as follows:

Process	Arrival Time	Start time	Finish time	Waiting time	Turnaround time
P1	10:00	10:00	12:00	0	2 hours
P2	10:10	12:00	13:00	1.50	2.90 hours
P3	10:25	13:00	13:25	2.35	3 hours

$$\text{Average Turnaround Time} = \frac{2+2.90+3.0}{3} = 2.63\,\text{hours}$$

Consider following set of processes that arrive at same time, with length of CPU burst time in given milliseconds

Process	Burst Time
P1	24
P2	3
P3	3

Therefore,

Process	Burst Time	Waiting time	Turnaround time
P1	24	0	24
P2	3	24	27
P3	3	27	30

Gantt Chart

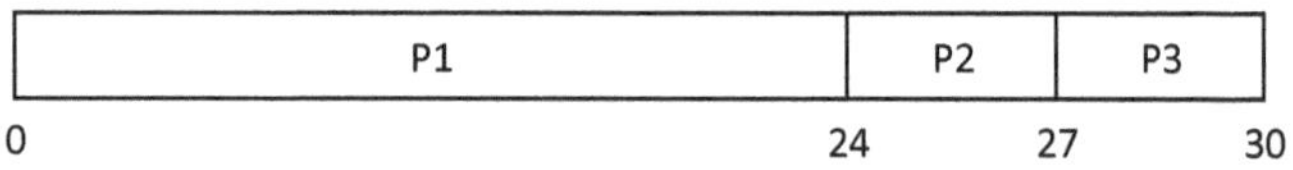

$$\text{Average Waiting Time} = \frac{0+24+27}{3} = 17\text{ms}$$

Drawbacks

i) Waiting time for processes is intolerable.

In the previous example waiting time for P3 is 27 ms and average waiting time is 17 ms. It is reduced if the processes are executed in P3, P2, P1 order.

Process	Burst Time	Waiting time	Turnaround time
P3	3	0	3
P2	3	3	6
P1	24	6	30

$$\text{Average Waiting Time} = \frac{0+3+6}{3} = 3\text{ms}$$

ii) The FCFS algorithm is particularly troublesome for time sharing systems where each user needs to get a share of CPU at regular interval. It would be disastrous to allow one process to keep CPU for an extended period.

3.2.2 Shortest Job First (SJF)

In this policy, the process with shorted expected processing time is selected next for execution. If two processes have same expected processing time, then FCFS scheduling is used to break tie.

Consider the following set of processes

Process	Burst Time
P1	6
P2	8
P3	7
P4	3

Therefore,

Process	Burst Time	Waiting time	Turnaround time
P4	3	0	3
P1	6	3	9
P3	7	9	16
P2	8	16	24

Gantt Chart

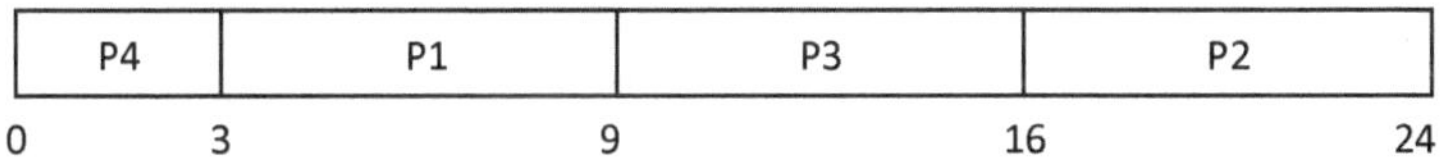

$$\text{Average Waiting Time} = \frac{3+16+9+0}{4} = 7\,\text{ms}$$

In the case of FCFS average waiting time would be 10.25.

Note: It is a non pre-emptive scheduling policy. Whenever, this algorithm is used, scheduler is invoked whenever job is completed or running process surrenders control to OS.

Advantage

Optimal scheduling discipline in terms of minimizing the average waiting time of given work load.

Drawbacks

i) It needs to know or at least estimate the required processing time for each process.

ii) Possibility of starvation for longer processes as long as there is a steady supply of shorter processes.

iii) It is not desirable for time-sharing or transaction processing environment because of lack of pre-emption.

3.3.3 Shortest Remaining Time Next (SRTN)

It is the pre-emptive version of SJF. In this policy, whenever, an even occurs which makes a new process ready, the scheduler is invoked to compare the remaining CPU execution time for running process, with the time needed to complete newly ready process. Depending on outcome, running process may continue, or it may be pre-empted by the shortest remaining time process. If pre-empted, the running process joins ready queue.

Consider following set of processes.

Process	Arrival Time	Burst time
P1	0	8
P2	1	4
P3	2	9
P4	3	5

Therefore,

Process	Arrival Time	Burst Time	Waiting time	Turnaround time
P1	0	8	9	17
P2	1	4	0	4
P3	2	9	15	24
P4	3	5	2	7

Gantt Chart

P1	P2	P2	P2	P2	P4	P4	P4	P4	P4	P1	P1	P1	P1	P1	P1	P1	P3	P3	P3	P3	P3	P3	P3	P3	P3

0 1 2 3 4 5 6 7 8 9 10 11 12 13 14 15 16 17 18 19 20 21 22 23 24 25 26

3.3.4 Round Robin Scheduling

The Round Robin Scheduling is designed especially for time sharing systems. It is similar to FCFS scheduling, but pre-emption is added to switch between processes.

A small unit of time, called time quantum (time slice) is defined. A time quantum is generally from 10 to 100 miliseconds. The ready queue is used as circular queue.

To implement the round robin scheduling, we keep the ready queue as a FIFO queue of processes. New processes are added to the tail of ready queue. The CPU scheduler picks the first process from ready queue, sets a timer to interrupt after one time quantum, and dispatches the process.

Therefore, one of the following two things is possible:

i) If process has CPU burst of less than 1 time quantum, it releases the CPU voluntarily, then scheduler proceeds to next process in ready queue.

ii) If CPU burst of currently running process is longer than one quantum, the timer will go off and will cause an interrupt to OS. A context switch will be executed and process will be put at tail of ready queue. The scheduler will then select next process in ready queue.

Consider the following set of processes

Process	Burst time
P1	24
P2	3
P3	3

Time Quantum = 4 ms

Gantt Chart

P1	P2	P3	P1

0 4 7 10 30

Process	Burst Time	Waiting time	Turnaround time
P1	24	0+6=6	30
P2	3	4	7
P3	3	7	10

$$\text{Average waiting time} = \frac{6+4+7}{3} = 5.67$$

Note: If there are n processes in ready queue and time quantum is q.

i) Each process gets $\frac{1}{n \times q}$ quantum in chunk of at most q time units for example, if 5 processes and quantum is of 20 ms then in total 20 time quantum each process gets 1/5 × 20 = 4 time quantum.

ii) Each process must wait no longer than (n-1) × q time.

Note:

i) The performance of Round Robin algorithm depends heavily on the size of time quanta.

ii) If the quantum is very large RR policy is the same as FCFS policy.

iii) If the quantum is very small, the RR approach is called processor sharing appears to the user as through n processes has its own processor running at 1/n the speed of real processor.

iv) If the quantum is very short, processes move through the system quickly, thus involves significant overhead due to context switching. For example, if there is a process of 10 ms.

   if time quantum is 11 ms
      no overhead
   if time quantum is 6 ms
      1 context switch occurs
   if time quantum is 1 ms
      9 context switch occurs

Thus too short quantum slows down the execution of process.

3.3.5 Highest Response Ratio Next (HRRN)

This scheme is derived from SJF method and avoids the danger of starvation for large processors.

It derives dynamic priority value based on estimated execution time and incurred waiting time. This dynamic priority is known as response ratio which is derived as

$$\text{Response Ratio (RR)} = \frac{\text{Waiting time} + \text{expected execution time}}{\text{expected execution time}}$$

Note: Minimum value for RR is 1 which occurs when a process first enters the system.

In this scheduling algorithm, when current process completes or is blocked, scheduler picks the ready process with greatest value of response ratio. Is technique guarantees that job cannot be starved since the waiting time is also affecting the RR.

3.3.6 Priority Scheduling

A priority is associated with each process and CPU is allocated to the process with highest priority. Equal priority processes are scheduled in FCFS order.

Priority can be defined either internally or externally. Internally defined priorities use some measurable quantity or quantities to compute the priority of a process. For example, time limits, memory requirements, number of open files. External priorities are set by criteria that are external to OS such as importance of process, type and amount of funds being paid for computer use and so on.

Generally the priority range from 127 (low) to 0 (high).

Consider the following set of processes

Process	Burst time	Priority
P1	10	3
P2	1	1
P3	2	4
P4	1	5
P5	5	2

Gantt Chart

P1	P5	P1	P3	P4

0 1 6 16 18 19

Example: Consider the following set of processes

Process	Burst time	Priority
P1	10	3
P2	1	1
P3	2	3
P4	1	4
P5	5	2

Find the turnaround time and waiting time for each process for FCFS, SJF, RR and priority scheduling algorithm. (Quantum = 1)

Solution:

Gantt Chart for FCFS

P1	P2	P3	P4	P5

0 10 11 13 14 19

Process	Burst time	Waiting time	Turnaround time
P1	10	0	10
P2	1	10	11
P3	2	11	13
P4	1	13	14
P5	5	14	19

$$\text{Average waiting time} = \frac{0+10+11+13+14}{5} = \frac{48}{5} = 9.6$$

Gantt Chart for SJF

P2	P4	P3	P5	P1

0 1 2 4 9 19

Process	Burst time	Waiting time	Turnaround time
P1	1	0	1
P2	1	1	2
P3	2	2	4
P4	5	4	9
P5	10	9	19

$$\text{Average waiting time} = \frac{0+1+2+4+9}{5} = \frac{16}{5} = 3.2$$

Gantt Chart for RR

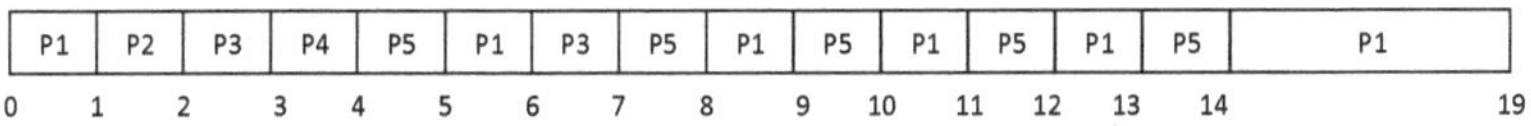

Process	Burst time	Waiting time	Turnaround time
P1	10	0+4+2+1+1+1+=9	19
P2	1	1	2
P3	2	2+3=5	7
P4	1	3	4
P5	5	4+2+1+1+1=9	14

$$\text{Average waiting time} = \frac{9+1+5+3+9}{5} = \frac{27}{5} = 5.4$$

Gantt Chart for Priority Algorithm

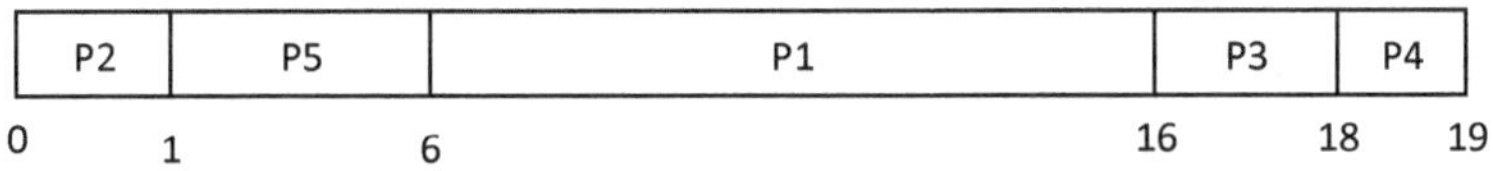

Process	Burst time	Waiting time	TA time
P1	16	6	16
P2	1	0	1
P3	2	16	18
P4	1	18	19
P5	5	1	6

$$\text{Average waiting time} = \frac{6+0+16+18+1}{5} = \frac{41}{5} = 8.2$$

3.3.7 Multiple Level Queue Scheduling

Multilevel queue scheduling algorithm partitions the ready queue into several separate queues. Processes are assigned to one queue, generally based on some property of process such as memory size, process priority or process type. Each queue is serviced by scheduling discipline best suited to the type of workload that it contains.

For example, separate queues for foreground and background processes. The foreground queue might be scheduled by RR algorithm while background queue is scheduled by FCFS algorithm.

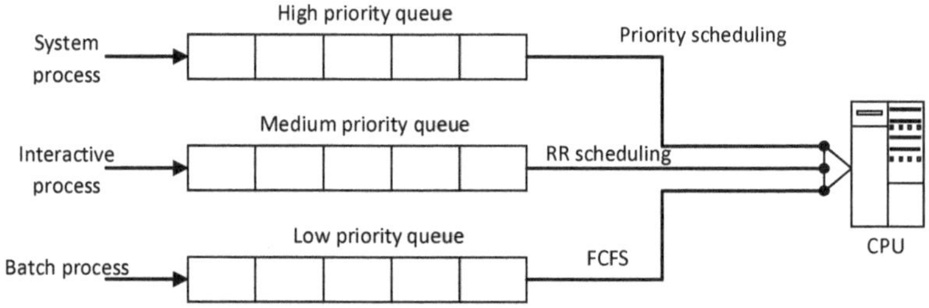

Figure 3.7: Multiple Level Queue Scheduling

In a single processor environment, some discipline must be devised for scheduling between queues.

Typical approaches are:

i) **Absolute Priority:** In the absolute priority case, the processes from the highest priority queue are serviced until that queue becomes empty. When highest priority queue becomes empty next queue may be serviced using its own scheduling algorithm. A lower priority process may be pre-empted by a higher priority process arrival in one of the upper level queue.

ii) **Time Slicing:** In the slicing approach certain percentage of processor time is assigned to each queue commensurate with its priority. For example, 40% of CPU time can be assigned to system process queue, 40% to interactive process queue and 20% to batch process queue.

3.3.8 Multiprocessor Scheduling

In the multiprocessor environment, one of the following two approaches can be used.

1) First approach tells that each processor is self scheduling. Each processor examines the common ready queue and selects a process to execute.

   If we have multiple processors trying to access and update common data, appropriate mechanism must be used to avoid race condition in multiprocessor environment.

   We must ensure that two processors do not choose the same process.

2) The second approach avoids the above problem by appointing one processor as scheduler for other processors, thus creating master-slave structure.

3.3.9 Real Time Scheduling

Real time computing may be defined as that type of computing in which the correctness of the system depends not only on logical result of computation but also on the time of which results we produced.

In general, in a real time system some of the tasks are real time tasks and they have a certain degree of urgency to them. Such tasks can be classified as:

i) **Hard Real Time Task:** Such type of task must meet its deadline; otherwise it will cause undesirable damage or fatal error to system. Such types of tasks are submitted along with a statement of the amount of time in which it needs to complete or perform I/O.

ii) **Soft Real Time Task:** It has associated deadline, which is desirable but not mandatory. It still makes sense to schedule and complete the task even if it has passed its deadline.

iii) **Aperiodic or Periodic Task:** Aperiodic task has a deadline by which it must finish or start or it may have a constraint on both start and finish. In the case of periodic task, the requirement may be stated as "once per period T".

Note: Examples of current application of real time systems include control of laboratory experiments, air traffic control, telecommunication, military command and control system, controllers of robots, controllers in space station, undersea exploration etc.

3.4 Deadlocks

3.4.1 Introduction

A system consists of finite number of resources to be distributed among a number of competing processes. The resources may be the processor I/O channel, main and secondary memory, devices and data structures such as files, databases and semaphores.

Under the normal mode of operation a process must request a resource after using it. A process may request as many resources as it requires carrying out its designated task. Thus a process may utilize a resource in only following way.

i) **Request:** If the request can not be granted immediately, then the requesting process must wait until it becomes free.

ii) **Use:** The process can operate on resource.

iii) **Release:** Process releases the resource after performing the required task.

Note: The number of resource requested may not exceed the total number resources available in the system.

A process in multiprogramming environment is said in a state of deadlock if it is waiting for a particular event that will never occur. The event with which we are mainly concerned here are resource acquisition and release. Thus:

> "a process request resources, and if the resources are not available at that time, the process enters a wait state. It may happen that waiting process will never again change state, because the resources it has requested are held by other waiting process. This situation is called **deadlock**."

A system is said to be in deadlock if one or more processes are deadlocked.

Consider the following scenario:

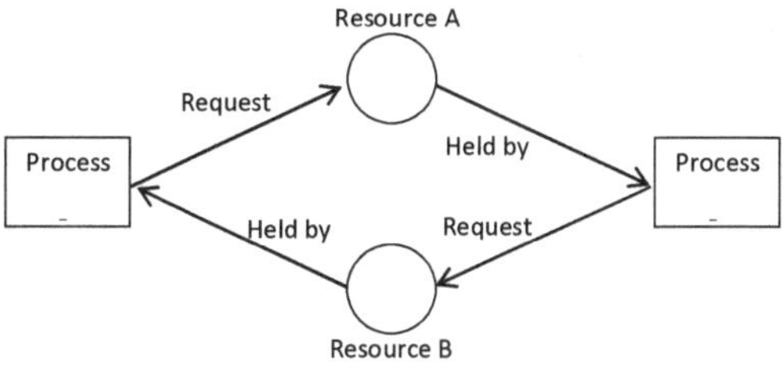

Figure 3.8: Deadlock scenario

A is allocated to P_2 and B is allocated to P_1. If P_1 request A and P_2 request B, then there will be a deadlock because A will be released only when P_2 gets B and B will be released only when P_1 gets A.

3.4.2 Deadlock Characterization

A deadlock situation can arise if the following four conditions hold simultaneously in a system.

i) **Mutual Exclusion:** Shared resources are acquired and used in mutual exclusive manner, that is, by at most one process at a time. If another process request that resource, it must be delayed until resource has been released.

ii) **Hold and Wait:** A process must be holding at least one resource and waiting to acquire additional resource that is currently being held by other process.

iii) **No Preemption:** Resources can not be preempted means; resources previously granted can not be forcibly taken away from a process. They must be explicitly released by the process holding them.

iv) **Circular Wait:** There is a circular chain of two or more processes, each of which is waiting for resources held by the next member of the chain.

All of these four conditions must be present for a deadlock to occur. If one of them is absent, no deadlock is possible.

3.4.3 Resource Allocation Graph

The resources are partitioned into several types, each of which consists of some number of identical instances. If the system has two CPUs then the resource type CPU has two instances. Similarly resource type printer may have five instances.

If a process requests an instance of resource type, allocation of any instance of the type will satisfy the request.

The resource allocation graph is used to determine deadlock in a system.

This graph consists of set of vertices V and set of edges E. The set of vertices V is partitioned into two different types of nodes as:

i) Set of all active processes in the system

ii) Set of all resource types in the system.

Then

Resource Allocation Graph = {V, E}

V = {P, R}

$P = \{P_1, P_2, P_3, P_4....\}$

$R = \{R_1, R_2, R_3......\}$

Edges

$P_i \rightarrow R_j$	Signifies that process P_i requested an instance of resource type R_j and is currently waiting for that resource. It is called request edge.
$R_j \rightarrow P_i$	Signifies that an instance of resource type R_j has been allocated to process P_i. It is called assignment edge.

In Resource Allocation Graph, process is represented as circle and each resource type as square. Since resource type may have more than one instance, such instances are represented as dot with in square.

Rules

When a process P_i requests an instance of resource type R_j, a request edge is inserted in Resource Allocation Graph. When this request can be fulfilled, the request edge is instantaneously transformed to assignment edge. When the process no longer needs access to the resource, it releases the resource and as a result assignment edge is deleted.

3.4.4 Conditions of Deadlock in Resource Allocation Graph

i) If each resource type has exactly one instance, then a cycle in Resource Allocation Graph implies that deadlock has occurred.

ii) If each resource type has several instances, then a cycle does not necessarily imply that a deadlock has occurred. In this case, a cycle in the graph is necessary but not sufficient condition for existence of deadlock.

Consider the following set of P, R and E.

$P = \{P_1, P_2, P_3,\}$

$R = \{R_1, R_2, R_3, R_4\}$

$E = \{P_1 \rightarrow R_1, P_2 \rightarrow R_3, R_1 \rightarrow P_2, R_2 \rightarrow P_2, R_2 \rightarrow P_1, R_3 \rightarrow P_3\}$

Resource Instances:

i) R_1 has one instances

ii) R_2 has two instances

iii) R_3 has one instances

iv) R_4 has three instances

There is no cycle in the graph so no process in the system is deadlocked.

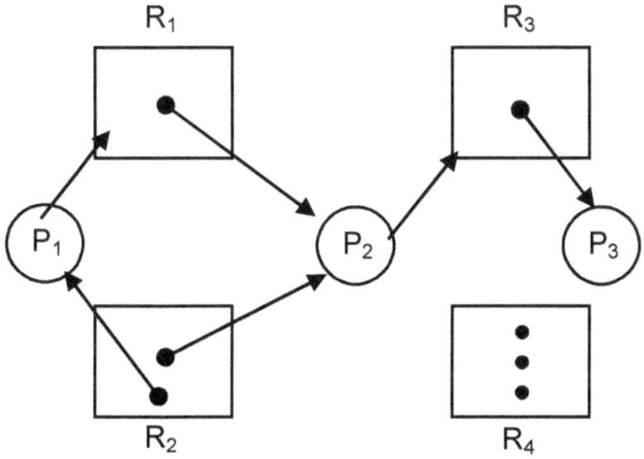

Figure 3.9: Resource Allocation Graph

Suppose process P_3 requests an instance of resource type R_2. Since no instance of R_2 is available, $P_3 \rightarrow R_2$ is added to graph. At this point two cycles exist in the system.

$$P_1 \rightarrow R_1 \rightarrow P_2 \rightarrow R_3 \rightarrow P_3 \rightarrow R_2 \rightarrow P_1$$
$$P_2 \rightarrow R_3 \rightarrow P_3 \rightarrow R_2 \rightarrow P_2$$

Here P_1, P_2 and P_3 are deadlocked because P_2 is waiting for the resource R_3 which is held by P_3. On the other hand P_3 is also waiting for either for P_1 or P_2 to release R_2. In addition P_1 is waiting for process P_2 to release R_1.

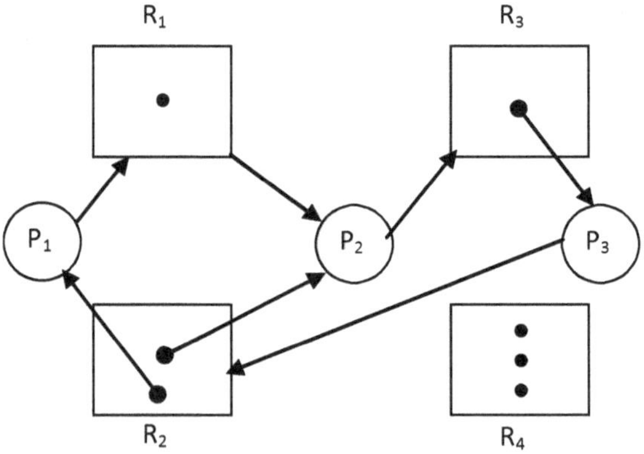

Consider another Resource Allocation Graph as shown in **figure below:**

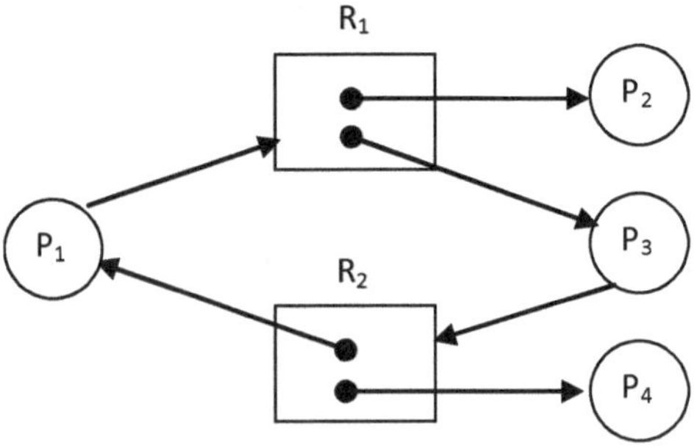

In this example there is a cycle:

$$P_1 \rightarrow R_1 \rightarrow P_3 \rightarrow R_2 \rightarrow P_1$$

But there is no deadlock because P_4 may release its instance of resource R_2 which can then be allocated to P_3, breaking the cycle.

3.4.5 Methods for Handling Deadlock

Principally, we can deal with deadlock problem in one of the three ways:

1) Deadlock Prevention
2) Deadlock Avoidance
3) Deadlock Detection and Recovery

3.4.5.1 Deadlock Prevention

The basic philosophy of deadlock prevention is to deny at least one of the four necessary conditions for deadlock. Let us elaborate on this approach by examining each of four necessary conditions.

i) **Mutual Exclusion:** In general, mutual exclusion for the resources cannot be disallowed because resources may be either sharable or non-sharable. For example, a printer cannot be simultaneously shared by several processes. On the other hand, sharable resources do not require mutually exclusive access. A process never needs to wait for sharable resource. For example read only files are sharable resources. If several processes attempt to open a read only file at the same time, they can be granted simultaneous access to the file.

   Thus mutual exclusion must be supported by OS if there are non-sharable resources in system.

ii) **Hold and Wait:** To ensure that the hold and wait condition never occurs in the system, we must guarantee that, whenever a process requests a resource, it does not hold any other resources.

   There are two approaches to prevent hold and wait condition:

   a) The process request all needed resources prior to commencement of execution. This strategy requires that all of the resources, a process will need, must be requested at once. The system must grant them on an "all or none" basis. If the set of resource needed by a process is available, then system may grant all of those resources to the process at one time and process will be allowed to proceed. If the complete set up resources needed by a process is not currently available, the process must wait until complete set is available.

b) The process requests resources incrementally in the course of execution but releases all its resource holding upon encountering a denial.

Note: First approach suffers following disadvantages:

- **Low Resource Utilization:** Since many resources may be allocated but remains unused for long time.
- **Starvation:** A process that needs several popular resources may have to wait indefinitely, because at least one of the resources that it needs is unavailable

ii) No Preemption: The no-preemption condition can be denied by allowing preemption, that is authorizing the system to revoke ownership of certain resource from blocked process. For this there are following approaches:

a) If a process is holding some resources and requests another resource that cannot be immediately allocated to it, then all the resources currently being held are preempted. The preempted resources are added to the list of resources for which process is waiting. The process will be restarted only when it can regain its old resources as well as new ones that it is requesting.

b) If a process requests, we first check whether they are available. If they are available allocate them. If they are not available, check whether they are allocated to some other process that is waiting for additional resources. If so, preempt the desired resources from waiting process and allocate them to requesting process. If the resources are not either available or held by a waiting process, requesting process must wait.

iii) Circular Wait: The circular wait condition can be prevented by defining a linear ordering of resource types and granting the resources in increasing order of enumeration.

In this approach all the resources are given a unique number in increasing order. Suppose R = {R_1, R_2, ..R_m}

If a process acquires resource R_j then it can only request resources R_{j+1} or higher thereafter.

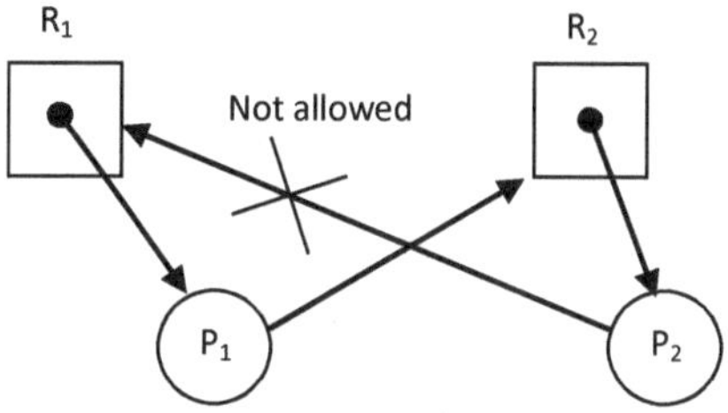

Figure 3.9: Circular wait prevention

3.4.5.2 Deadlock Avoidance

In the deadlock prevention, we constrain resource requests to prevent at least one of the four conditions of deadlock from occurring. This leads to:

i) Low resource utilization

ii) Reduced system throughput

iii) Starvation

The basic idea of deadlock avoidance is to grant only those requests for available resources that cannot possibly result in a state of deadlock. This strategy is usually implemented by having the resource allocator examine the effect of granting a particular request. If the granting of resource cannot possibly lead to deadlock, the resource is granted to requestor otherwise requesting process is suspended until such time when its pending request can be safety granted. Thus, this approach requites knowledge of future requests of resources.

Safe State: A state is safe if the system can allocate resources to each process in some order and still avoid deadlock. More formally, a system is in safe state only if there exists a safe sequence. A sequence of process $<P_1, P_2, P_3 .... P_n>$ is safe sequence for current allocation state if, for each P_i, the resources that P_i can still request can be satisfied by the currently available resources plus the resources held by all the P_j where $j < i$.

In this situation, if the resources that P_i needs are not immediately available, then P_i can wait until all P_j have finished. When they finished, P_i can obtain all of its needed resources, complete its designated task; return its allocated resources and terminate.

A safe state is not a deadlock state, but unsafe state may lead to deadlock.

Consider the following system with maximum 12 instances of resource and three processes P_0 P_1 P_2

Process	Maximum Need	Allocated	Need
P_0	10	5	5
P_1	4	2	2
P_2	9	2	7

Available instance of resource = 3

Above state is safe state because there exist a safe sequence $<P_1, P_0, P_2>$. Means P_1 is allocated all the needed instance of resource type, and when it completes it returns them. Now the system has 5 available instance of resource, which are allocated to P_0. After the completion of P_0, system has 10 instance of resource type from which 7 are allocated to P_2 and thus all processes complete.

Note: A system may go from safe state to unsafe state. Suppose at any time P_2 request a resource and it is allocated to it then.

Process	Maximum Need	Allocated	Need
P_0	10	5	5
P_1	4	2	2
P_2	9	3	6

Available instance = 2

Now no safe sequence is possible because only P_1 can be allocated all the need resource instances and when it returns, system has 4 available resources which are not sufficient enough to quench the thrust of either P_0 or P_2, so P_0 and P_2 will have to wait infinitely resulting to deadlock.

Consider the following example consisting of four processes and three resources. The total instances of resources R_1, R_2 and R_3 are 9, 3, and 6.

The maximum need of processes and current allocation state is given below:

	P_1	P_2	P_3	P_4
R_1	3	6	3	4
R_2	2	1	1	2
R_3	2	3	4	2

Total Claim Matrix

	P_1	P_2	P_3	P_4
R_1	1	6	2	0
R_2	0	1	1	0
R_3	0	2	1	2

Current Allocation Matrix

R_1	0
R_2	1
R_3	1

Available Vector

To answer the question "is this a safe state?", we ask an immediate question "can any of four processes be run to completion with the resources available?". Means "Is any safe sequence possible?".

Yes in the above example a safe sequence <P_2, P_1, P_3, P_4> is possible, which is shown below:

Allocate all the resources needed to P_2

	P_1	P_2	P_3	P_4
R_1	3	0	1	4
R_2	2	0	0	2
R_3	2	0	3	0

Claim Matrix

	P_1	P_2	P_3	P_4
R_1	1	6	2	0
R_2	0	1	1	0
R_3	0	3	1	2

Current Allocation Matrix

R_1	0
R_2	1
R_3	0

Available Vector

After completion of P_2

	P_1	P_2	P_3	P_4
R_1	3	0	1	4
R_2	2	0	0	2
R_3	2	0	3	0

Claim Matrix

	P_1	P_2	P_3	P_4
R_1	1	0	2	0
R_2	0	0	1	0
R_3	0	0	1	2

Current Allocation Matrix

R_1	6
R_2	2
R_3	3

Available Vector

Allocate all the resources to P_1

	P_1	P_2	P_3	P_4
R_1	0	0	1	4
R_2	0	0	0	2
R_3	0	0	3	0

Claim Matrix

	P_1	P_2	P_3	P_4
R_1	3	0	2	0
R_2	2	0	1	0
R_3	2	0	1	2

Current Allocation Matrix

R_1	4
R_2	0
R_3	1

Available Vector

After completion of P_2 allocate resources needed to P_3

	P_1	P_2	P_3	P_4
R_1	0	0	0	4
R_2	0	0	0	2
R_3	0	0	0	0

Claim Matrix

	P_1	P_2	P_3	P_4
R_1	0	0	3	0
R_2	0	0	1	0
R_3	0	0	4	2

Current Allocation Matrix

R_1	6
R_2	2
R_3	0

Available Vector

After completion of P_3 all the resources needed by P_4 may be allocated to P_4 thus all the processes complete with available resources.

Example of Unsafe State

Consider the state defined by the following matrix:

	P_1	P_2	P_3	P_4
R_1	3	6	3	4
R_2	2	1	1	2
R_3	2	3	4	2

Claim Matrix

	P_1	P_2	P_3	P_4
R_1	1	5	2	0
R_2	0	1	1	0
R_3	0	1	1	2

Allocation Matri

R_1	1
x R_2	1
R_3	2

Available Vector

i) Suppose P_2 makes request for 1 unit of R_1 and 1 unit of R_3. If we assume that request is granted, then resulting state is same as in previous example, which is in safe state.

ii) Suppose P_1 makes the request for 1 unit of R_1 and R_3 and if we assume that request is granted we are left in following state

	P_1	P_2	P_3	P_4
R_1	3	6	3	4
R_2	2	1	1	2
R_3	2	3	4	2

Claim Matrix

	P_1	P_2	P_3	P_4
R_1	2	5	2	0
R_2	0	1	1	0
R_3	1	1	1	2

Allocation Matrix

R_1	0
R_2	1
R_3	1

Available Vector

This is an unsafe state because each process requires at least one additional unit of R and none is available. Thus no safe sequence is possible.

The concept of safe and unsafe state suggest a deadlock avoidance strategy, which is to ensure that system of processes and resources be always in safe state. To achieve this following strategy is used.

"When a process makes a request for a set of resources, assume that request is granted update the system state accordingly and then determine if the result is safe state". If so, grant the request, if not, block the process until it is safe to grant the request.

Note: A safe state is not a deadlock state but a deadlock state is an unsafe state. All the unsafe states are not deadlock state but an unsafe state may lead to deadlock state, which is shown below.

It is just because in an unsafe state a process may release some resources which it does not require currently. If that happened, system may return to safe state.

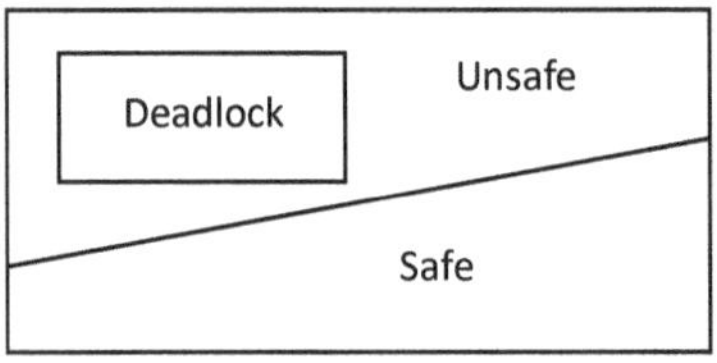

Thus, the deadlock avoidance strategy does not predict deadlock with certainty, it merely anticipates the possibility of deadlock and assumes that there is never such a possibility.

Algorithms for Deadlock Avoidance

Using the concept of safe state, we can define avoidance algorithms that ensure that system will never deadlock. The idea is "Whenever a process request a resource that is currently available, the system must decide whether the resource can be allocated immediately or whether the process must wait. The request is granted only if the allocation leaves the system in safe state".

Resource Allocation Graph Algorithm

This algorithm is used in the system with only one instance of each resource.

Method: In addition to request and assignment edges, a new edge called claim edge is introduced in this algorithm. This edge is represented by dashed edge. Before the process P_i starts executing, it must claim all the resources a priori in the system, i.e., all the claim edges of a process must appear in Resource Allocation Graph before it starts executing. A claim edge $P_i \rightarrow P_i$ just indicates that process P_i may request R_i at same time in future. Whenever, P_i requests resource R_j, the claim edge $P_i \rightarrow P_j$ is converted in request edge. Similarly when a resource R_j is released by P_i, assignment edge is reconverted to claim edge $P_j \rightarrow R_j$.

Rule: The request can be granted only if converting the request edge $P_i \rightarrow R_j$ to an assignment edge does not result in formation of cycle in resource allocation graph.

Example: Suppose P_1 and P_2 both requires R_1 and R_2 to complete its task.

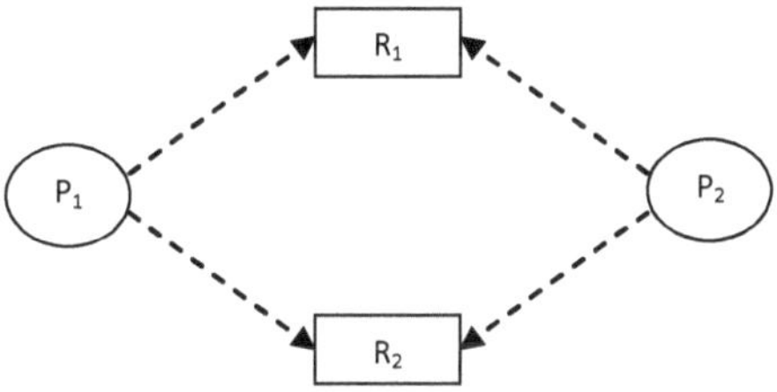

Initial State

First P_1 makes the request for R_1 it is granted.

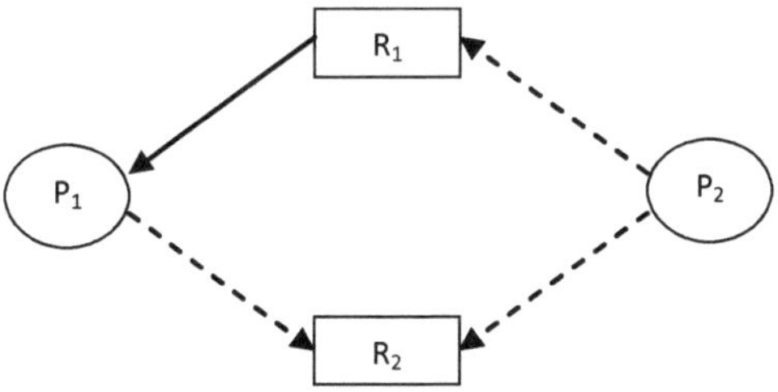

Now if P_2 makes request for R_1 it is converted into request edge.

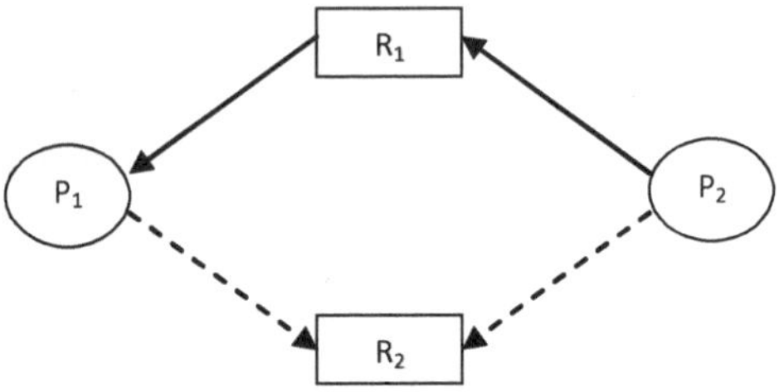

Now if P_2 makes the request for R_2, although R_2 is available but it cannot be granted to P_2 since this action will create cycle in graph.

Disadvantage: This approach is not applicable to resource allocation system with multiple instance of each resource type.

Banker's Algorithm

The name for this algorithm was chosen because this algorithm can be used in banking system to ensure that bank never allocates its available cash such that it can no longer satisfy the need of its all customers.

Several data structures are maintained to implement banker's algorithm. These data structure encode the state of resource allocation system.

Let **n** be the number of processes in the system and **m** be the resource type. We need following data structure:

i) **Available:** A vector of length **m** indicates the number of available resource of each type.

ii) **Max:** An n × m matrix defines the maximum demand of each process. If max[i, j] = k then process P_i may request at most **k** instance of resource type R_j.

iii) **Allocation:** An n × m matrix defines the number of resource of each type currently allocated to each process. If Allocation [i, j] = k, then process P_j is currently allocated the k instance of resource type R_j.

iv) **Need:** An n × m matrix indicates the remaining need of each process. If Need [i, j] = k then process P_i may need k more instance of resources type R_j to complete its task.

Need [i, j] = Max [i, j] – Allocation [i, j]

These data structure vary over time in both size and value. These data structures are used by following algorithms which are the part of Banker's algorithm.

Request-Resource Algorithm

Let, $Request_i$ be the request vector of P_i. If $Request_i$ [j] = k, then process P_i want k instance of R_j. When request is made by P_i, the following action is taken.

Step 1: If $Request_i$ £ $Need_j$, go to step 2; otherwise raise an error condition since the process has exceeded its maximum claim.

Step 2: If $Request_j$ £ Available, go to step 3; otherwise P_i must wait since the resources are not available.

Step 3: Have the system pretend that it has allocated the requested resource to P_i by modifying the state as follows:

Available = Available – $Request_i$
$Allocation_i$ = $Allocation_i$ + $Request_i$
$Need_i$ = $Need_i$ – $Request_i$

If the resulting state is safe, process is allocated it's resources. However, if the new state is unsafe, P_i must wait for $request_i$ and old allocation state is restored.

The resulting state is safe or not, it is determined by following Safety Algorithm.

Safety Algorithm

Step 1: Let Work and Finish be vectors of length m and n respectively.

Initialize
Work = Available
Finish [i] = false

For i = 1, 2, ... n

Step 2: Find an i such that both

a) Finish [i] = false
b) $Need_i \le Work$
If no such i exist go to step 4.

Step 3: $Work = Work + Allocation_j$
Finish [i] = True
Go to step 2.

Step 4: If finish [i] = true for all i, the system is in safe state.

Example: Consider the following scenario:

	Max				Allocation			Available		
	A	B	C		A	B	C	A	B	C
P_0	7	5	3	P_0	0	1	0	3	3	2
P_1	3	2	2	P_1	2	0	0			
P_2	9	0	2	P_2	3	0	2			
P_3	2	2	2	P_3	2	1	1			
P_4	4	3	3	P_4	0	0	2			

The matrix Need can be determined

Need = Max – Allocation

	Need		
	A	B	C
P_0	7	4	3
P_1	1	2	2
P_2	6	0	0
P_3	0	1	1
P_4	4	3	1

The above system is in safe state because by using the Banker's safety algorithm the sequence $<P_1, P_3, P_4, P_2, P_0>$ satisfy the safety criteria.

Now suppose P_1 request one additional instance of A and two instances of C, so $Request_j = (1, 0, 2)$. To decide whether this request can be immediately granted, we first check that $Request_j$ < Available means (1, 0, 2) £ (3, 3, 2), which is true, then we pretend that this request has been fulfilled and we arrive at the following state.

	Allocation				Need			Available		
	A	B	C		A	B	C	A	B	C
P_0	0	1	0	P_0	7	4	3	2	3	0
P_1	3	0	2	P_1	0	2	0			
P_2	3	0	2	P_2	6	0	0			
P_3	2	1	1	P_3	0	1	1			
P_4	0	0	2	P_4	4	3	1			

To determine this new system state is safe. Banker's safety algorithm is executed. As the sequence $<P_1, P_3, P_4, P_6, P_2>$ satisfies the safety requirement.

Hence request of Pi is immediately granted.

3.4.5.3 Deadlock Detection and Recovery

Deadlock detection is the process of actually determining that deadlock exists and of identifying the process and resources involved in deadlock.

In this strategy resources are granted to requesting process without any check. Periodically system state is examined to determine if a set of processes is deadlocked.

The algorithm that examines the state of system whether the deadlock has occurred, are described below:

Wait-for Graph: This algorithm is used in systems where each resource has single instance.

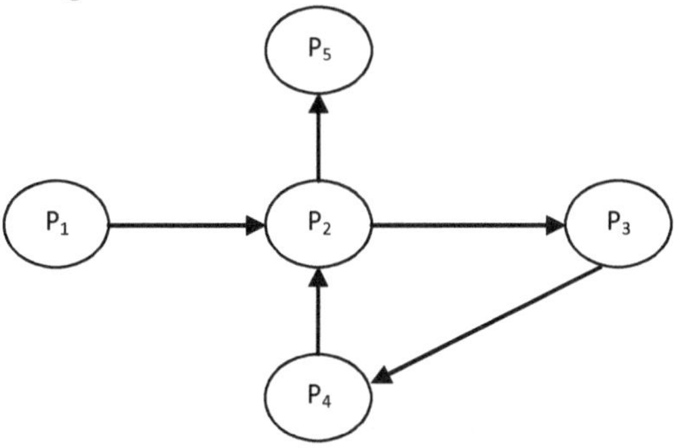

Figure 3.10: A Wait-for Graph with Deadlock

An edge from P_i to P_j ($P_i \rightarrow P_j$) in wait for graph implies that process P_i is waiting for P_j to release resource that P_i needs.

A deadlock exists in the system if and only if the wait-for graph contains cycle. To detect deadlocks, the system needs to maintain the wait for graph and periodically to invoke an algorithm that searches for a cycle in graph.

Algorithm for Several Instances of Resource Type

This deadlock detection algorithm employs several time-varying data structures:

i) **Available:** A vector of length **m** indicates the number of available resources of each type.

ii) **Allocation:** An n × m matrix defines the number of resources of each type currently allocated to each process.

iii) **Request:** An n × m matrix indicates the current request of each process. If Request [i, j] = k, then Process P_j requesting k instance of R_j.

Deadlock Detection Algorithm

Step 1: Let Work and Finish be vector of length m and n respectively. Initialize

Work = Available

If Alllocation_i ¹ 0, then Finish [i] = false

otherwise, Finish[i] = true

for i = 1, 2, ...n

Step 2: Find an index i such that both

Finish[i] = false

Request_i £ Work

Step 3: If no such i exists, go to step 5.

Step 4: Work = Work + Allocation_i

Finish[i] = true

Go to step 2

Step 5: If F[i] = false, for some i, 1 £ i £ n then system is in deadlock state. Moreover, if Finish [i] = false, then P_i is deadlocked.

To illustrate the algorithm consider the following system state:

	Allocation				Request			Available		
	A	B	C		A	B	C	A	B	C
P_0	0	1	0	P_0	0	0	0	0	0	0
P_1	2	0	0	P_1	2	0	2			
P_2	3	0	3	P_2	0	0	0			
P_3	2	1	1	P_3	1	0	0			
P_4	0	0	2	P_4	0	0	2			

After execution of deadlock detection algorithm, we find that sequence <P_0, P_2, P_3, P_1, P_4> will result in Finish[i] = true for all i. So system is in not deadlock state.

Suppose now P_2 makes one additional request for an instance of C, the request is

	Request		
	A	B	C
P_0	0	0	0
P_1	2	0	2
P_2	0	0	1
P_3	1	0	0
P_4	0	0	2

Now, system is now deadlocked. The deadlocked processes are P_1, P_2, P_3, P_4.

When to invoke deadlock algorithm:

i) Periodically

ii) Whenever a request for a resource has to wait

iii) In special circumstances such that whenever CPU utilization drops below 40%.

Recovery from Deadlock

After detection the deadlock, the recovery can be made in following ways:

1) **By aborting Processes:** Process can be aborted in following manner:
   i) Abort all deadlocked processes.
   ii) Abort one process at a time until the deadlock cycle is eliminated.
2) **Selecting the victim**: Aborting all the deadlocked processes is not good approach so a process whose abortion costs minimum is selected as victim and that process is aborted. A process is selected as victim by considering following facts:
   i) In which order should we choose to abort?
   ii) Priority of the process.
   iii) How long process has computed, and how much longer to completion?
   iv) Resources the process has used.
   v) Resources process needs to complete.
   vi) How many processes will need to be terminated?
   vii) Is process interactive or batch?
3) **Rollback:** As aborting and restarting process costs much so the victim process can be rolled back to some previous safe state so that some resources can be preempted.
4) **Starvation:** While selecting a process as victim it should be taken into consideration that a process should not be selected as victim so many times otherwise it will face the starvation.

PRACTICE QUESTIONS

Subjective Questions:

Q.1. How Banker's Algorithm is used for Deadlock avoidance?

Q.2. Round-robin scheduling behaves differently depending on its time quantum. Can the time quantum be set to make round robin behave the same as following:

- FCFS
- SJF

Q.3. What are the performance criteria for CPU scheduling algorithms?

Q.4. Explain Process Control Block? Where and by whom is it maintained?

Q.5. Differentiate among short-term, medium-term and long term Scheduling.

Q.6. Is there a deadlock in given snap shot of systems [Figure (a) and figure (b)]? Justify your answer also.

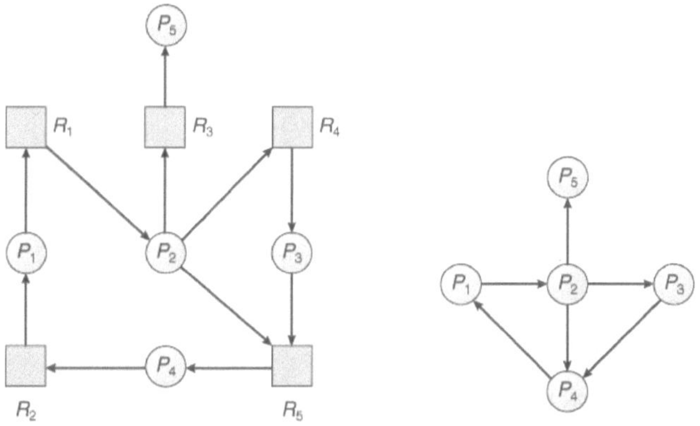

(a) (b)

Q.7. Discuss the term

- Wait for graph
- Resource allocation graph

Q.8. How does deadlock prevention differ from deadlock avoidance?

Q.9. What are the similarities and differences between starvation and deadlock?

Q.10. Consider the following snapshot of the system.

Process	Allocation	Max	Available
	A B C D	A B C D	A B C D
P0	0 0 1 2	0 0 1 2	1 5 2 0
P1	1 0 0 0	1 7 5 0	
P2	1 3 5 4	2 3 5 6	
P3	0 6 3 2	0 6 5 6	
P4	0 0 1 4	0 6 5 6	

- What is the content of Need Matrix
- Is the system currently in safe state? If yes, give the safe sequence.
- If request from P1 arrives for (0,4,2,0), can the request be granted immediately?

Q.11. An operating system uses Shortest Remaining Time first (SRT) process scheduling algorithm. Consider the arrival times and execution times for the following processes:

Process	Execution time	Arrival time
P1	19	0
P2	24	14
P3	9	29
P4	14	44

Compute the average waiting time and average turnaround time of the processes.

Q.12. Consider the following set of processes.

Processes	P1	P2	P3	P4	P5
Arrival Time	0	2	4	5	7
Burst Time	10	6	4	4	6
Priority	9	7	6	7	5

Where Priority is defined as 0>1>2>3>.........

Draw the Gantt chart and calculate the Average waiting time and turnaround time for Preemptive Priority and Non Preemptive priority Scheduling.

Q.13. Consider the following snapshot of the system.

Process	Allocation	Request	Available
	A B C	A B C	A B C
P0	2 2 3	3 6 8	4 3 3
P1	0 1 1	4 3 3	
P2	1 2 4	3 4 4	

- Is the system currently in deadlocked state? If no, give the safe sequence.
- If theP1 requests for one instance of A and one instance of B, can the request be granted immediately?

Q.14. Explain the term indefinite postponement? How does it differ from deadlock? How is it similar?

Q.15. For the following set of processes calculate average turnaround time and waiting time using SJF and Preemptive SJF scheduling

Processes	Arrival time	Burst time
P1	0	1
P2	2	8
P3	3	4
P4	6	5
P5	4	10
P6	9	12

Short Answer Type Questions:

Q.1. A CPU scheduling algorithm determines an order for the execution of its scheduled processes. Given n processes to be scheduled on one processor, how many possible different schedules are there? Give a formula in terms of n.

Q.2. Is a non-preemptive scheduling algorithm a good choice for an interactive system? Justify your answer.

Q.3. Prove that the safety algorithm presented in deadlock requires an order of m x n2 operations.

Short Answer Type Questions:

Q.1. What is meant by Process-ID ?

Q.2. What is Preemptive Scheduling?

Q.3. How the hold & wait conditioned can be prevented?

Q.4. When a system is called in usafe state?

Q.5. What is the disadvantage of invoking the detection algorithm for every request?

Q.6. What are the disadvantages of FCFS Scheduling?

Q.7. Which of the scheduling algorithms gives minimum average waiting time ?

Q.8. What is the responsibility of long term scheduler?

Q.9. What are turnaround time and response time?

Q.10. What is Gantt Chart?

CHAPTER

4

Memory Allocation

4.1 Introduction

Memory management is the functionality of an operating system which handles or manages primary memory and moves processes back and forth between main memory and disk during execution. Memory management keeps track of each and every memory location, regardless of either it is allocated to some process or it is free. It checks how much memory is to be allocated to processes. It decides which process will get memory at what time. It tracks whenever some memory gets freed or unallocated and correspondingly it updates the status.

The programs can be allocated the space in main memory by different methods as shown below:

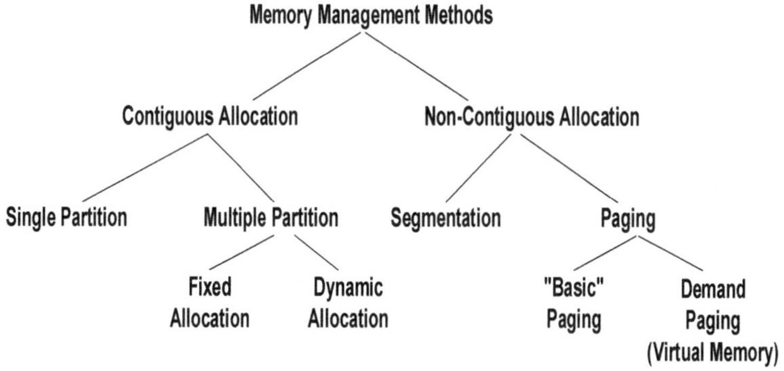

Figure 4.1 : Different methods for memory allocation

4.2 Contiguous Allocation

4.2.1 Memory Partitioning

To make the maximum advantage of multiprogramming it is necessary for several jobs to reside in computer's main memory at once. Thus when one job requests I/O, the CPU may be immediately switched to another.

To manage the user portion of main memory there are following two approaches

1) Fixed partitioning
2) Variable partitioning or Dynamic partitioning

1) Fixed Partitioning

The simplest scheme for managing the user portion of main memory is to partition it into regions with fixed boundaries. Each partition can hold a single job.

The size of partition may be either equal or unequal.

We use two schemes for fixed partition multiprogramming:

i) Absolute translation and loading
ii) Re-locatable translation and loading

i) **Absolute Translation and Loading:** In this approach, a job queue is maintained for each partition by OS as shown below.

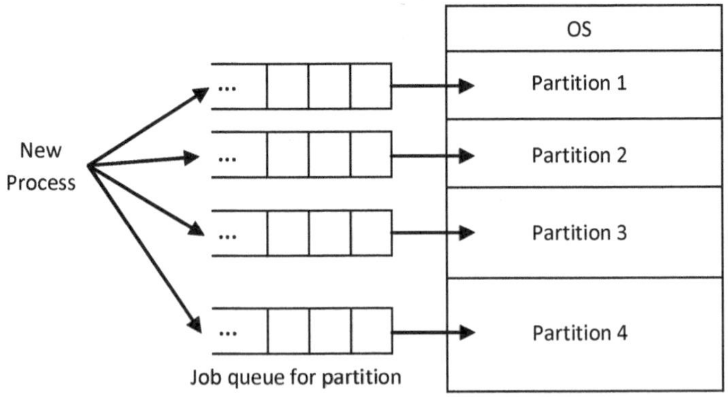

Figure 4.2: Absolute Translation and Loading

Drawbacks

a) Inefficient use of memory due to internal fragmentation (if the size of process is smaller than the size of partition, there is wastage of space internal to partition. It is known as internal fragmentation.

b) Maximum number of active processes is fixed (it is the number of partitions).

c) It may be possible that queue for large partition is empty while queue for small partition is containing many processes.

ii) Re-locatable Translation and Loading: In this approach a single queue is maintained for all the partitions. Whenever, a partition becomes free, it is filled by the job from job queue by using following approaches:

a) The job closest to front of the queue that fits it. Since it is undesirable to waste a large partition on small job thus following policy is used.

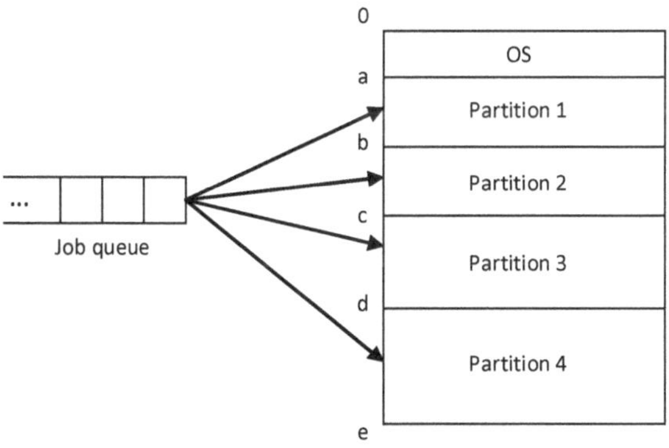

Figure 4.3 : Re-locatable Translation and Loading

b) The whole job queue is searched and best fit job for partition is loaded.

Since it gives the poor service to smaller jobs and it is desirable that the smallest job should be given the best service, not the worst. Therefore the following approach is used.

c) This approach has a rule that a job can not be skipped more than k times. Each time it is skipped, it gets one point, when it acquires k points, it can not be skipped.

2) Variable Partitioning or Dynamic Partitioning

With the dynamic partitioning, the partitions used are of variable length. When a process is brought into main memory, it is allocated exactly as much memory as it requires and no more.

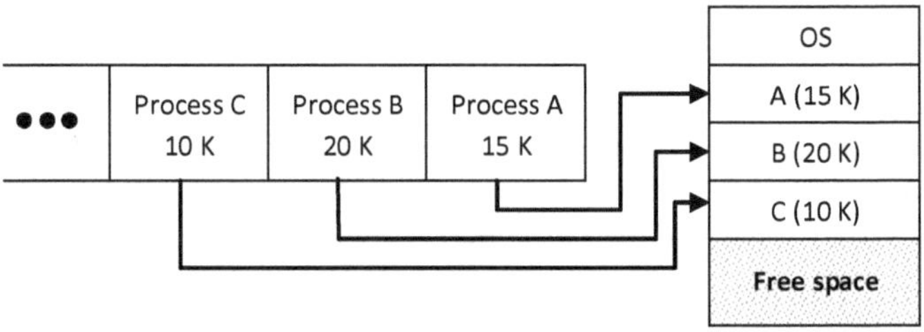

Figure 4.4: Variable Partitioning or Dynamic Partitioning

Whenever a job finishes its work it leaves a hole in memory. So, the completion of jobs leads to a situation in which there are a lot of small holes in memory. As time goes on, memory becomes more and more fragmented. This phenomenon is called external fragmentation.

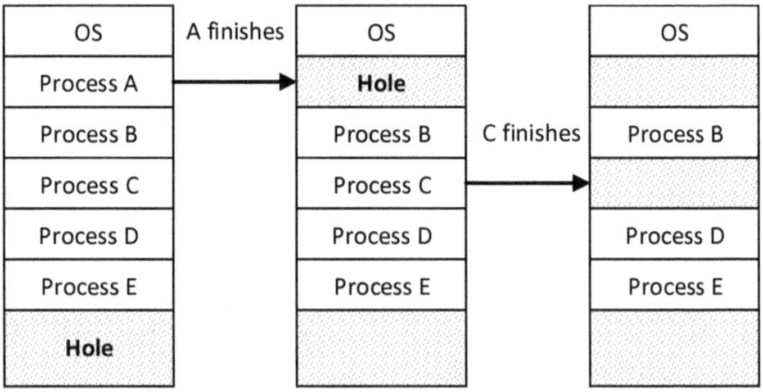

Figure 4.5: Effect of Dynamic Partitioning

Compaction: The technique for overcoming the external fragmentation is compaction. In this approach OS shifts the processes so that they are contiguous and so that free memory is together in one block.

So this technique involves moving all occupied area of storage to one end and this leaves a single large free storage hole instead of numerous small holes common in variable partitioning.

Sometime storage compaction is also known as garbage collection.

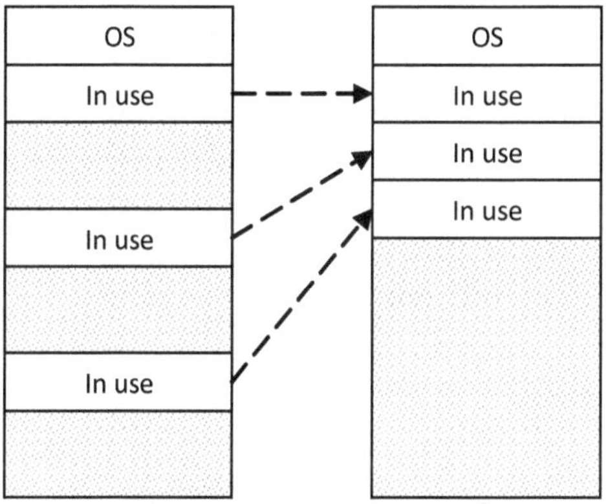

Figure 4.6: Effect of Compaction

Compaction is not without drawbacks.

i) It consumes system resources that could otherwise be used productively

ii) The system must stop everything while it performs compaction. It increases the response time.

iii) Compaction involves relocating jobs that are in main memory. This means relocation information must be modified.

4.2.2 Storage Placement Strategies

Because memory compaction is time consuming, the OS designer must be clever in deciding how to assign processes to memory (how to fill the holes). When there is a time to load or swap a process into main memory, and if there is more than one free block of memory of sufficient size, then OS must decide which free block to allocate by using following approaches:

i) **Best fit:** An incoming job is placed in the hole in main memory in which it fits tightly and leaves the smallest amount of unused space.

ii) **First fit:** An incoming job is placed in main storage in the first available hole large enough to hold it.

iii) **Worst fit:** An incoming job is placed in the hole in which it fits worst i.e., largest possible hole.

iv) **Next fit:** This approach begins to scan memory from the location of last placement and chooses the next available block that is large enough.

Consider the following example which uses the above approaches for an incoming new job of 16 m.

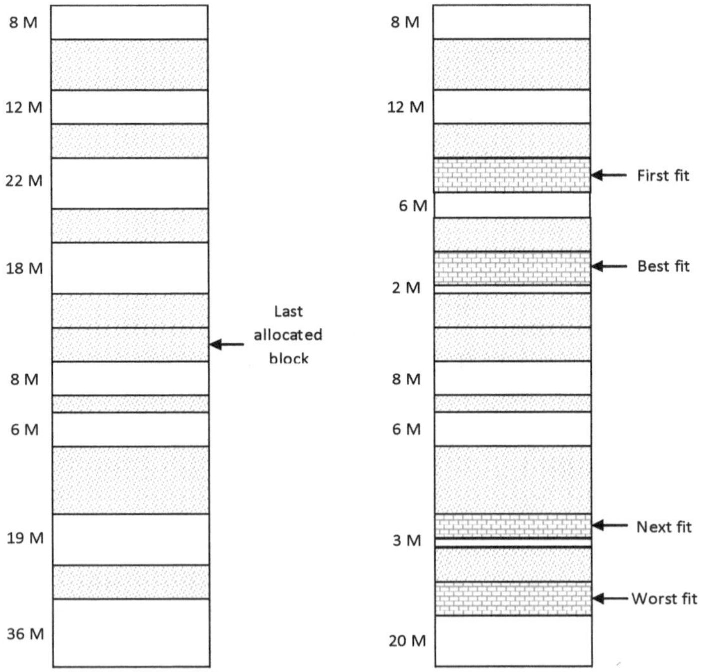

Figure 4.7 : Storage Placement Example

Relocation: In both approaches (dynamic and fixed partitioning) a process may occupy different partitions during the course of its life. When a process image is first created, it is loaded into some partition in main memory. Latter the process may be swapped out, when it is swapped in it may be assigned to different partition than the last time. Furthermore when compaction is used, processes are shifted while they are in main memory. Thus the location of process is not fixed. They will change each time a process is swapped in or shifted. To solve this problem a distinction is made among several types of address.

4.3 Non-Contiguous Allocation

4.3.1 Paging

Both the fixed and variable partitioning approaches are inefficient in the use of memory. They result in either external or internal fragmentation.

To overcome the above problem a new approach known as paging is used.

Main memory is divided into fixed size chunks known as frames. The size of frames is kept relatively small. Process is also divided into small fixed size chunks of same size. The chunks of process is known as pages.

At a given time some of the frames in memory are in use and some are free. A list of free frames is maintained by operating system. When it is time to load a process into the memory, OS finds the required free frames in memory and loads the pages of process in that frame.

The hardware support for paging is illustrated below.

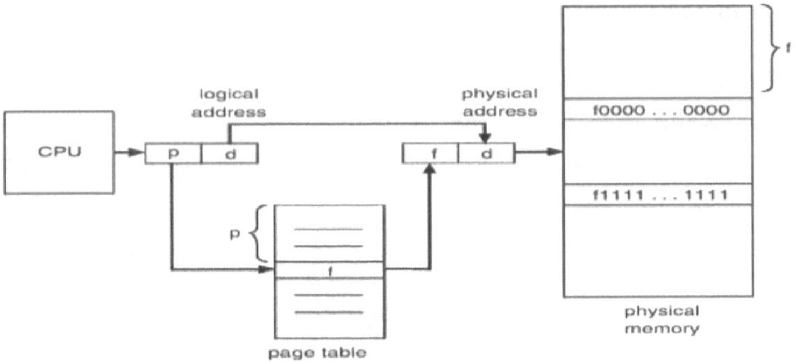

Figure 4.8: Paging Hardware

Consider process stored on disk, consists of four pages. When it comes time to load this process, the OS finds four free frames and loads the four pages of process A into four frames. Process B consisting of 3 pages, and process C consisting of four pages are subsequently loaded. Then the process B is suspended and swapped out of main memory. Latter all of the process in main memory are blocked and OS needs to bring a new process D consists of 5 pages. The scenario may be as follows:

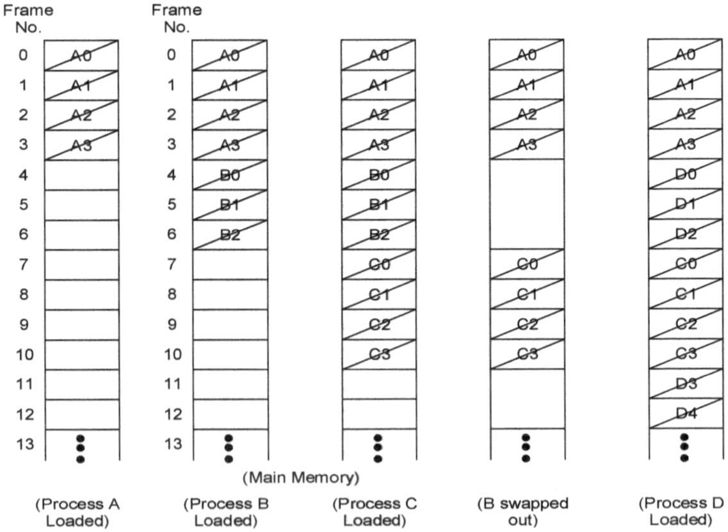

Figure 4.9: Pa®ging Example

Paging is a form of dynamic relocation. Every logical address is bound by paging hardware to some physical address. Using paging is similar to using table of base registers one for each frame of memory.

When a process arrives in the system to be executed, its size expressed in pages is examined. Each page of process needs one frame. Thus, if the process requires n pages, at least n pages must be available in memory. If n frames are available they are allocated to this arriving process. The first page is loaded into one of the allocated frames and frame number is put in the page table for this process. The next page is loaded into another frame and its page number is put into another frame and so on.

An important aspect of paging is clear separation between the user's view of memory and actual physical memory. The program views that memory as single contiguous space containing only this one program. In fact, the program is scattered throughout physical memory which also holds other program. The difference between the user's view of memory and actual physical memory is reconciled by address translation hardware.

The logical addresses are translated into physical address as follows:

If the size of process is 2^m and page size is 2^n addressing unit (byte or words) then high order (m – n) bits of logical address designate page number while low order n bits designate line number.

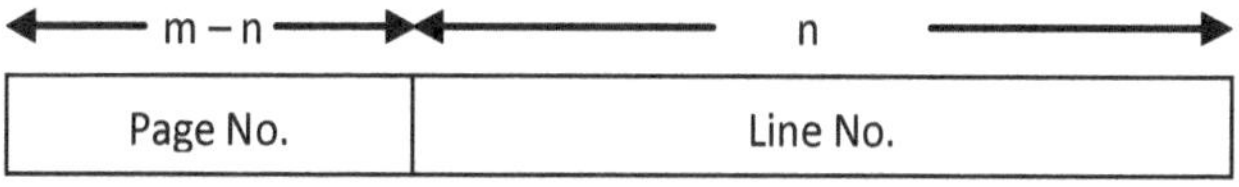

Logical Address

Let size of physical memory (Physical memory space) is 2^p

Then

Number of pages in process= Process size/Page Size = $\frac{2^m}{2^n}$

Number of frames in physical memory= Physical memory size/Frame size = $\frac{2^p}{2^n}$

[Note: Page size=Frame Size]

Following are steps for translating logical address into physical

i) Extract the page number as left-most m – n bits of logical address.

ii) Use this page number as index into process table to find the frame number (f).

iii) The starting address of the frame is $f \times 2^n$. Physical address is reference by that number plus line number.

If size of process is 4K (2^{12}) and block(Page/Frame) size is K (2^{10}) and physical memory size is 8K

Then

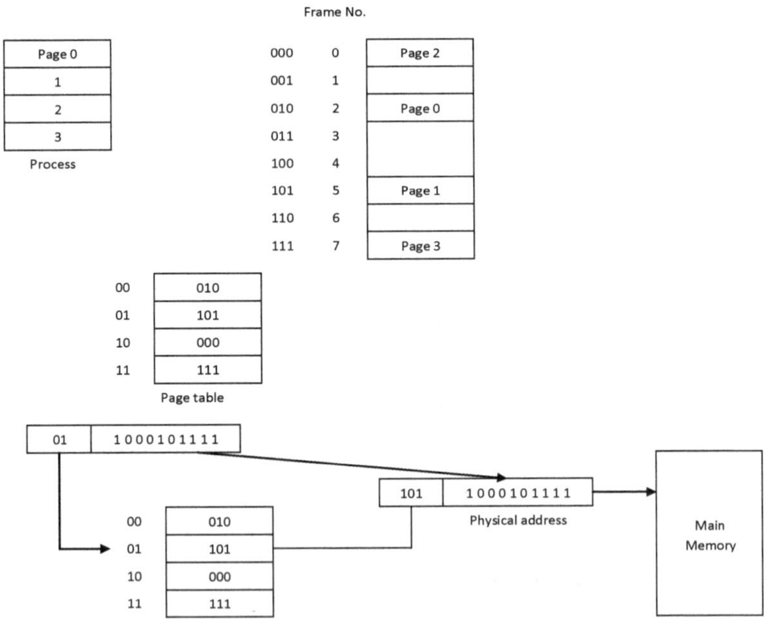

Figure 4.10 : Paging illustration

Example A

Consider a logical address space of eight pages of 1024 words each mapped on to a physical memory of 32 frames. Find out the number of bits in logical address and the number of bits in physical address.

Answer

Size of logical address space = 8 pages

Page size = 1024 words

Therefore, size logical address space in words $= 8 \times 1024$ words

$= 2^3 \times 2^{10}$

$= 2^{13}$ words

So bits in the logical address = 13

Size of physical address space = 32 frame

As we know that page and frame has same size

So size of physical address space in words $= 32 \times 1024$ words

$= 2^5 \times 2^{10}$ words

$= 2^{15}$ words

So bits in physical address = 15.

Example B

Consider a paged logical address space (composed of 32 pages of 2 Kbytes each) mapped into a 1 Mbyte physical memory space.

i) What is the format of processor's logical address?

ii) What is the length and width of page table?

iii) What is the effect on the page table if the physical memory space is reduced by half?

Answer

i) Size of logical address space = 32 pages

Page size = 2 KB = 2×1024 words

So size of logical address space in words = $32 \times 2 \times 1024$ words

$= 2^5 \times 2 \times 2^{10}$ words

$= 2^{16}$ words

So logical address has 16 bits

ii) As we know that

Number of words in page table = number of pages in logical address space

Therefore page table has 32 words

As we know that page size is equal to frame size. So, Frame size = 2×1024

So number of frames in physical memory

$$= \frac{\text{Physical Memory Space}}{\text{Frame Size}}$$

$$= \frac{1 \times 1024 \times 1024}{2 \times 1024} = 512 = 2^9$$

Bits in each word of page table = bits required to address all frames in physical memory = 9

iii) If the physical memory is reduced by half then number of frames in physical memory will be 2^8

Thus page table will have 32 words each of 8 bits.

4.3.2 Segmentation

The fixed page size used in paging causes certain difficulties with respect to program size and the logical structure of programs. It is more convenient to divide programs and data into logical parts called segments. A segment is set of logically related instruction or data element associated with given name. Segments may be generated by programmer or by OS.

Note: Under the paging system, process subdivisions are physical entities, not related to the logical structure of process in any intentional way. However, the segments in a segmentation scheme correspond to logical division of process.

A user's view of program may be

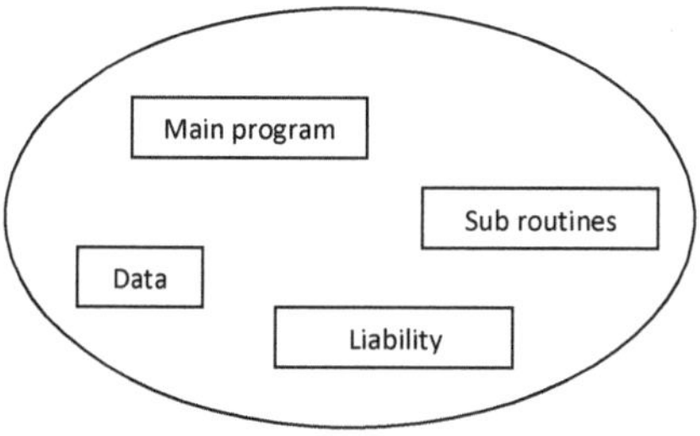

Figure 4.11: User's view of program

Segmentation is a memory management scheme that supports this user view. A logical address space is a collection of segments. Each segment has a name and length.

Segment Addressing

A logical address consist of two fields.

<segment number, offset>

Segment number indexes a process segment table. Each entry in segment table has segment base and segment limit. Segment base contains the physical address where segment resides in memory, whereas segment limit specifies the length of segment. The use of segment table is shown below

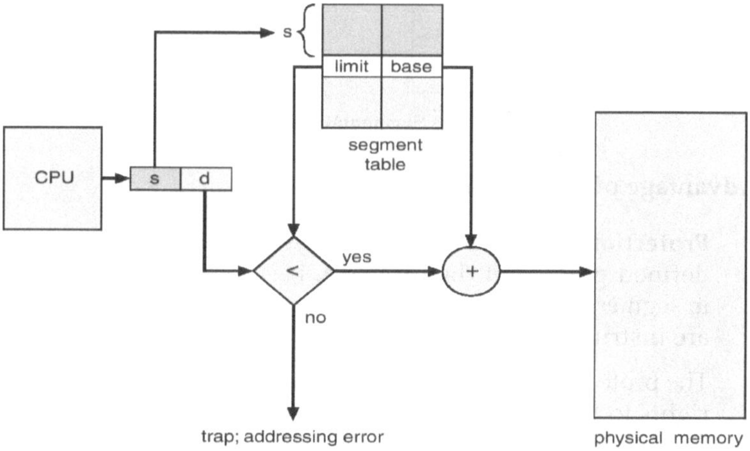

Figure 4.12: Segmentation Hardware

A logical address consists of two part:

i) A segment number (s)

ii) Offset (d)

The segment number is used as an index into segment table. The offset d of logical address must be between 0 and segment limit. If it is not, we trap to OS (logical addressing beyond end of segment). If the offset is legal it is added to segment base to produce the physical address.

Example of Segmentation

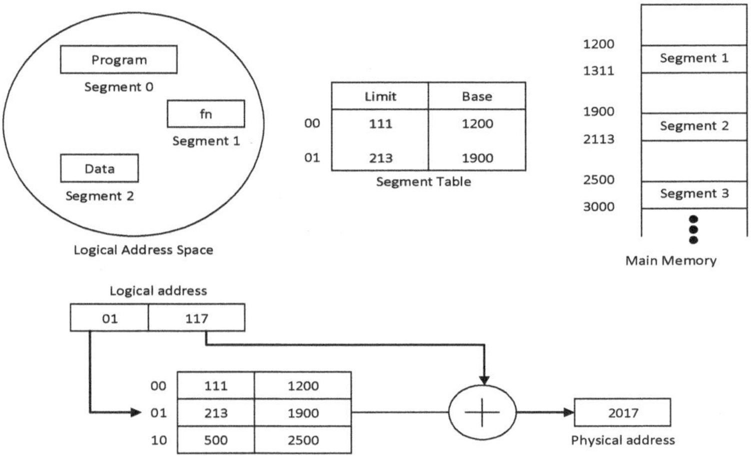

Figure 4.13 : Segmentation Example

Advantage of Segmentation

i) Protection: Because the segments represent a semantically defined portion of the program, it is likely that all entries in segment will be used the same way. Hence, some segments are instructions while other segments are data.

The protection field in segment table entry specifies the access rights to the particular segment.

Limit	Base	Protection

The protection information is set into the segment table by master control program of OS. Some of the access rights of interest that are used for protecting the programs.

a) Full read and write privileges
b) Read only (write protected)
c) Execute only (program protection)
d) System files

a) Full read and write privileges are given to program when it is executing its own instructions.
b) Write protection is useful for sharing system programs such as utility programs and other library routines. These system programs are stored in area of memory where they can be shared by many users. They can be read by all programs but no writing is allowed.
c) The execute only condition protects program from being copied. It allows the user to execute the segment program instructions but prevents them from reading the instruction as data for purpose of copying their content.

ii) **Sharing:** Segments are shared when entities in segment tables of two different processes point to same physical locations.

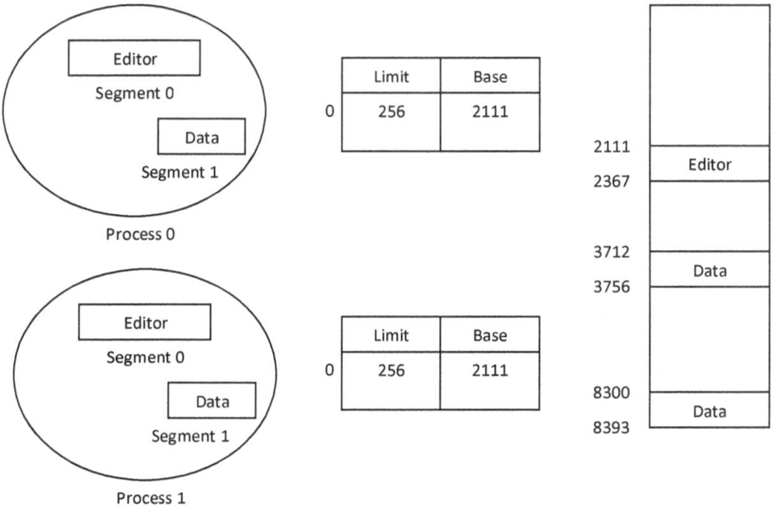

Figure 4.14 : Sharing in Segmentation

4.3.3 Segmentation with Paging

Both paging and segmentation have their strengths. Paging, which is transparent to the programmer, eliminates external fragmentation and thus provides efficient use of main memory. Pieces that are moved in and out of main memory are of fixed equal size, it is possible to develop sophisticated memory-management algorithms that exploit the behavior of programs.

Segmentation is visible to the programmer and has the ability to handle growing data structures, modularity, and support for sharing and protection. To combine the advantages of both, some systems are equipped with processor hardware and operating system software to provide both.

In a combined paging/segmentation system process is devided into a number of segments at the discretion of the programmer. Each segment is in turn broken up into a number of fixed-size pages which are equal in length to a main memory frame. If a segment is less than a page in length, the segment occupies just one page. From the programmer's point of view, a logical address still consists of a segment number and a segment offset. From the system's point of view, the segment offset is viewed as a page number and page offset for a page within the specified segment. Thus the logical address is partitioned into three fields. The segment field specifies the segment number. The page field specifies the page within segment and word field specifies the specific word within the page.

Segment	Page	Word

Logical Address

Presented with a virtual address, the processor uses the segment number portion to index into the process segment table to find the page table for that segment. Then, the page number portion of the virtual address is used to index the page table and look up the corresponding frame number. This combined with the offset portion of the virtual address to produce the desired real address.

The mapping of logical address into a physical address is done by means of two tables as below:

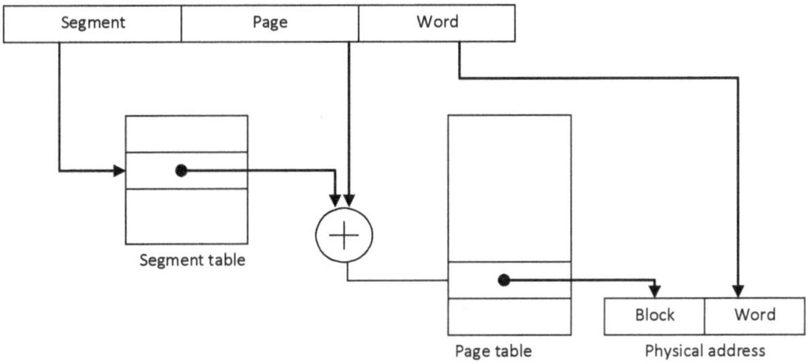

Figure 4.15: Segmentation with Paging

The segment number of the logical address specifies the address for the segment table. The entry in the segment table is a pointer address for page table base.

This page table base is added to the page number given in the logical address. The sum produces a pointer address to an entry in page table. The value found in page table provides a frame number in physical memory. The concatenation of the frame field with the word field produces the final physical mapped address.

Consider 20 bit logical address

4	8	8
Segment	Page	Word

4 bit segment number specifies 16 possible segments. 8 bit page number can specify upto 256 pages and 8 bit word field implies a page size of 256 words.

This configuration allows each segment to have any number of pages upto 256. The smallest possible segment will have one page or 256 words. The largest possible segment will have 256 pages means 256 × 256 = 64 K words.

Consider a segment of program is to be loaded into the memory and that requires 5 pages. The OS may assign segment number 6 to it. When it is loaded into physical memory, it is distributed among five blocks in physical memory where the OS finds empty space.

4.4 Virtual Memory

The memory management schemes that we have seen so far are necessary because of one basic requirement: The instructions being executed by the processor must be in the physical memory of the machine. The first approach to meeting this requirement was to place the entire logical address space (i.e., the entire process) into the main memory. Comparing simple paging and simple segmentation, on one hand, with fixed and dynamic partitioning, on the other, we have the foundations for a more sophisticated memory management system.

There are two characteristics of paging and segmentation which are key:

- All memory references within a process are logical addresses that are dynamically translated into physical addresses at run time. This means that a process can be swapped in and out of main memory such that it occupies different regions of main memory at different times during its lifetime.
- A process may be broken up into a number of chunks (either pages or segments) and these chunks need not be contiguously located in main memory during execution. The combination of dynamic run-time address translation and the use of a page or segment table permit this.

Putting these two key elements together allows us to realize that it is not necessary that all of the pages or segments of a process be in main memory during execution. If the page or segment that holds the next instruction to be fetched and the page or segment that holds the next data location to be accessed, are both in main memory, then at least for a time, the execution may proceed.

The ability to execute a program that is only partially in main memory provides many benefits, some of which are:

✓ A program is no longer constrained in size by the amount of physical memory. Programmers could write programs for a very large virtual address space.

✓ The degree of multiprogramming can be increases since each user program could take less physical memory.

✓ Less I/O is required to load or swap each user program into memory, so the program would execute faster.

Virtual memory involves the separation of logical memory as perceived by users from the physical memory. This separation allows an extremely large virtual memory to be provided for programmers when only a much smaller physical memory is available. The following illustrates the basic concept of virtual memory.

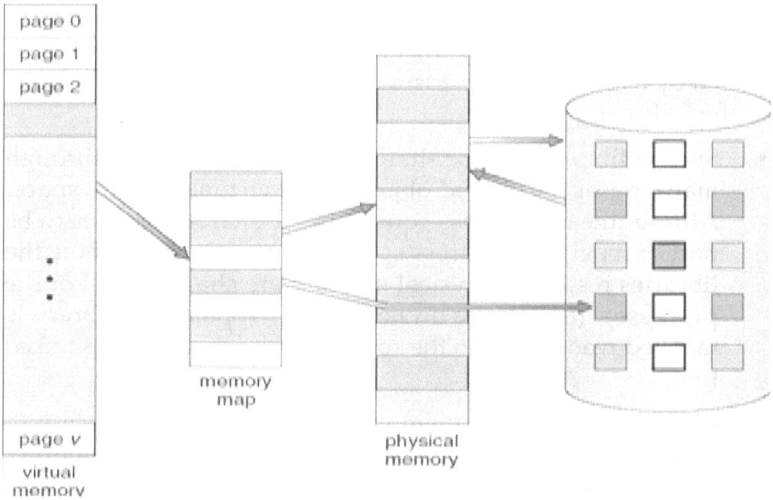

Figure 4.16: Virtual Memory that is Larger Than Physical Memory

The virtual address space of a process refers to the logical (or virtual) view of how a process is stored in memory. The following figure illustrates the virtual address space of a process.

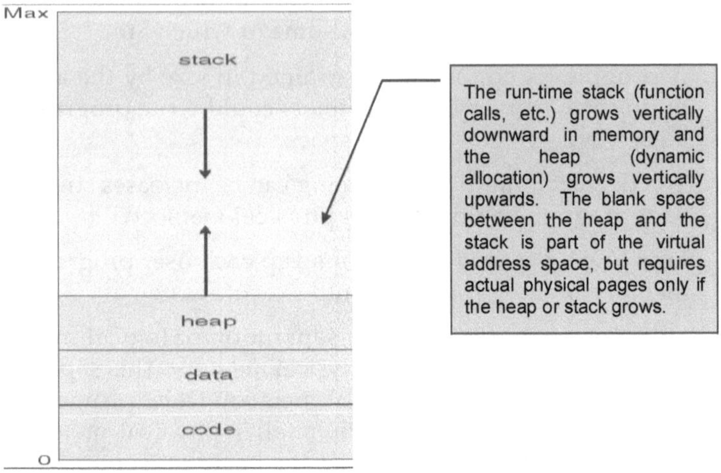

Figure 4.17: Virtual-address Space

In addition to separating logical memory from physical memory, virtual memory also allows files and memory to be shared by two or more processes through page sharing. This leads to the following benefits:

- System libraries can be shared by several processes through mapping of the shared object into a virtual address space. Although each process considers the shared libraries to be part of its virtual address space, the actual pages where the libraries reside in physical memory are shared by all of the processes. (See figure on next page.) Typically, a library is mapped read-only into the space of each process that is linked to it.
- Processes can share memory, by allowing one process to create a region of memory that it can share with another process. Processes sharing this region consider it part of their virtual address space, yet the actual physical pages of memory are shared.
- Virtual memory can allow pages to be shared during process creation with the fork() system call, thus speeding up process creation.

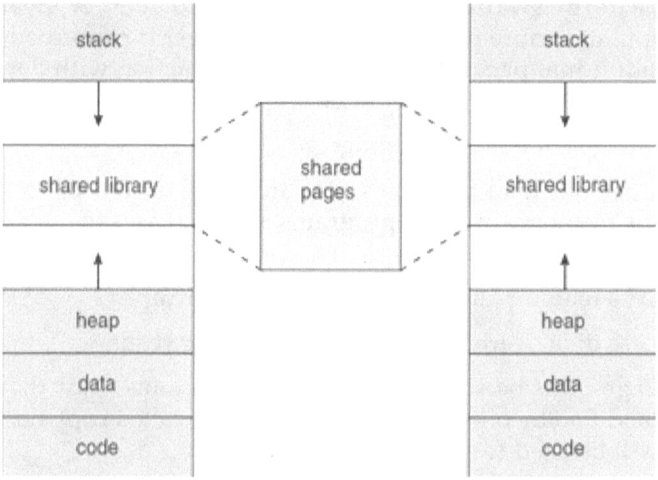

Figure 4.18: Shared Library Using Virtual Memory

Implementation of Virtual Memory

Virtual memory is implemented by demand paging, i.e., parts of user program expressed in pages are loaded into system memory if required. Demand segmentation can also be used to provide virtual memory. Because of the variable-sized feature of segments the associated segment replacement algorithms are more complex than page replacement algorithms.

4.4.1 Demand Paging

Demand paging is a simple method of implementing virtual memory. In a system that uses demand paging, the operating system copies a page into physical memory only if an attempt is made to access it (*i.e.*, if a page fault occurs). It follows that a process begins execution with none of its pages in physical memory, and many page faults will occur until most of a process's working set of pages is located in physical memory. This is an example of lazy loading techniques. A lazy swapper never swaps a page into memory unless that page will be needed.

Note: Since we are now viewing a process as a sequence of pages, rather than as one large contiguous address space, use of the term swapper is technically incorrect. A swapper manipulates entire processes, whereas a pager is concerned with the individual pages of a process. In conjunction with demand paging the term pager should be employed.

Advantages of demand paging:

- Does not load the pages that are never accessed, so saves the memory for other programs and increases the degree of multiprogramming.
- Less loading latency at the program startup.
- Less disk overhead because of less page reads.
- Pages will be shared by multiple programs until they are modified by one of them, so a technique called copy on write will be used to save more resources.
- Ability to run large programs on the machine, even though it does not have sufficient memory to run the program. This method is better than an old technique called overlays.
- Does not need extra hardware support than what paging needs, since protection fault can be used to get page fault.

Disadvantages:

- Individual programs face extra latency when they access a page for the first time. So prepaging, a method of remembering which pages a process used when it last executed and preloading few of them, is used to improve performance.
- Memory management with page replacement algorithms becomes slightly more complex.

Since a page is loaded into main memory only when it is needed, the question arises as to how does the system know when a page is needed? A page is needed whenever a program statement makes a reference (addresses a location) to a page. When a reference is made to a page one of three situations will arise:

- The referenced page is already in main memory. Action: do nothing.

- The referenced page is not already in main memory. Action: load page.
- The reference is invalid (out of range, etc.). Action: abort process

When a process is to be swapped in, the pager "guesses" which pages will be used before the process is swapped out again. By swapping in only those pages that will be used, the swap time is decreased, as is the amount of main memory that is required.

However hardware support is required to distinguish the pages that are in memory and those that are on the disk (backing store). The valid-invalid bit scheme is used for that. In this scheme a extra bit known as valid-invalid bit is added with each entry of page table. With demand paging, if the bit is set to "valid", the associated page is both legal (within the logical address space of the process) and in memory. If the bit is set to "invalid", the page is either not within the logical address space of the process or is a valid address but is currently not in the main memory (i.e., it is on the disk).

A page table entry for a page that is currently in memory is set in the same manner as with the simple paging scheme, but the page table entry for a page that is not currently in memory is either simply marked invalid, or contains the address of the page on disk.

This is illustrated in the following figure.

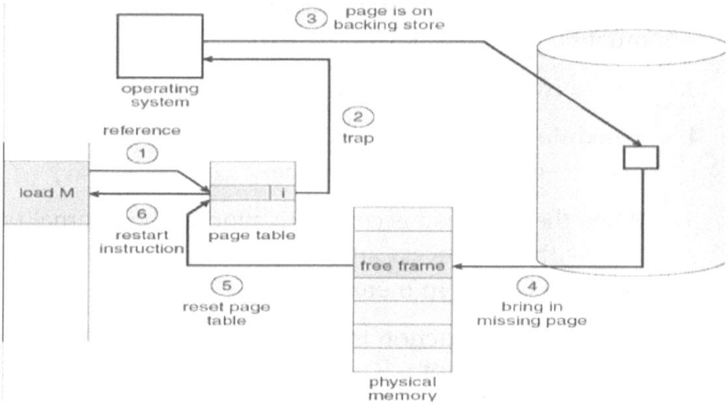

Figure 4.19: Demand paging

4.4.2 Page Faults:

Notice that marking a page invalid will have no effect if the process never attempts to reference that page. Thus, if the pager guesses correctly and pages in only those pages that are actually needed, the process will run exactly as though all of its pages had been loaded. As long as the process executes and references pages that are memory resident, execution will proceed normally.

What happens if the process references a page that is not memory resident? A page-fault occurs.

A page-fault occurs whenever the paging hardware, in translating the logical address through the page table, encounters the invalid bit set. This generates a page-fault trap. This trap is the result of the OS's failure to bring the desired page into memory.

The procedure for handling a page-fault is straightforward and consists of the following steps:

1. Check an internal table (usually maintained with the PCB) for this process to determine whether the reference was a valid or invalid memory reference.
2. If the reference was invalid, terminate the process. If it was valid, but the page is not resident in memory, it must be paged in now.
3. Find a free frame in memory.
4. Schedule a disk operation (I/O) to read the desired page into the newly allocated frame.
5. When the disk read is complete, modify the internal table kept with the process and the page table to indicate that the page is now in memory.
6. Restart the instruction that was interrupted by the page-fault. The process will now access the page as though it had always been in memory.

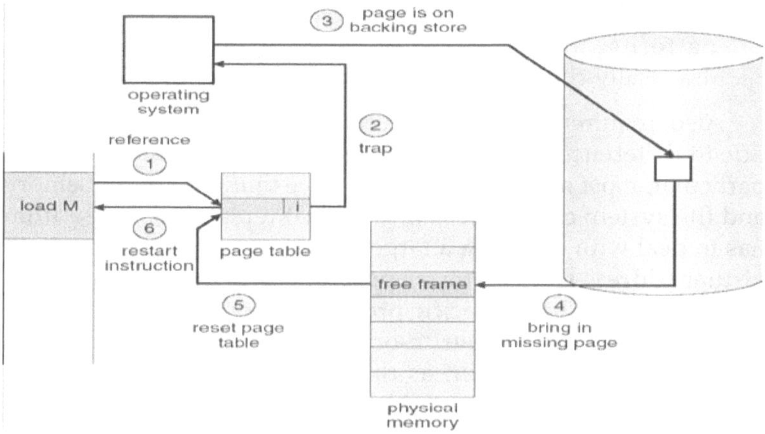

Figure 4.20: Page Fault

4.5 Page Replacement Policies

Replacement algorithms were a hot topic of research and debate in the 1960s and 1970s. That mostly ended with the development of sophisticated LRU approximations and working set algorithm. Since then, however, some basic assumptions made by the traditional page replacement algorithms were to some degree invalidated, resulting in revival of research in that area. In particular, the following trends in the behavior of underlying hardware and user-level software affected performance of replacement algorithms:

- Size of primary storage increased by multiple orders of magnitude. With several gigabytes of primary memory, algorithms that require periodic check of each and every memory frame are becoming less and less practical.
- Memory hierarchies grew taller. The cost of CPU cache miss is far more expensive. This exacerbates the previous problem.
- Locality of reference of user software has weakened. This is mostly attributed to the spread of Object-oriented programming techniques that favor large number of small functions, use of sophisticated data structures like tree and

Hash table that tend to result in chaotic memory reference patterns, and the advent of garbage collection that drastically changed memory access behavior of applications.

Also, requirements for replacement algorithms have changed due to differences in operating system kernel architectures. In particular, most modern OS kernels have unified virtual memory and file system caches. This means, that replacement algorithm has to deal with selecting a target page among pages from both virtual address spaces of user programs and from cached files. The latter pages have specific properties. For example, they can be locked, or can have write-ordering requirements imposed by journalling. Moreover, as the goal of page replacement is to minimize total time wasted by waiting for memory, it has to take into account memory requirements imposed by other kernel sub-systems that allocate memory. As a result, in modern kernels (Linux, FreeBSD, and Solaris) page replacement tends work at the level of low-level general-purpose kernel memory allocator, rather than at the level of virtual memory subsystem proper.

4.5.1 Local vs. Global Replacement

Replacement algorithm can be *local* or *global*. When a process incurs a page fault, a local page replacement algorithm selects for replacement some page that belongs to that same process (or a group of processes sharing memory partition). A global replacement algorithm is free to select any page in memory.

Local page replacement assumes some form of memory partitioning that determines how many pages are to be assigned to a given process of a group of processes. Most popular forms of partitioning are *fixed partitioning* and *balance set* algorithm based on the working set model. Advantage of local page replacement is its scalability: each process can handle its page faults independently without contending for some shared global data structure.

4.5.2 Precleaning

Most replacement algorithms simply return target page as their result. This means that if target page is *dirty* (that is, contains data that have to be written to the stable storage before page can be reclaimed), I/O has to be initiated to send that page to the stable storage (to *clean* the page). In the early days of virtual memory, time wasted on cleaning wasn't of much concerns, because virtual memory was first implemented on systems with full duplex channels to the stable storage, and cleaning was customarily overlapped with pagein. Contemporary commodity hardware, on the other hand, doesn't support full duplex transfers, and cleaning of target pages becomes an issue.

To deal with it various *precleaning* policies are implemented. Precleaning is mechanism that starts I/O on dirty pages that are (likely) to be replaced soon. Idea is that by the time precleaned page is actually selected for the replacement I/O will finish and page will be clean. Precleaning assumes that it is possible to identify pages that will be replaced *next*. Too eager precleaning can waste I/O bandwidth by writing pages that manage to get re-dirtied before being selected for replacement.

4.5.3 The Theoretically Optimal Page Replacement Algorithm

The theoretically optimal page replacement algorithm (also known as OPT or clairvoyant replacement algorithm) is an algorithm which works as follows: when a page needs to be swapped in, the operating system looks at all the pages currently in memory, and sees how long it is before that page will be used. Then, the operating system swaps out the page which will not be used longest. A page that is not going to be used until 6 million microseconds pass will be swapped out over a page which is going to be used after 4 thousand microseconds.

However, this algorithm cannot be implemented in the general purpose operating system, simply because it is not possible or feasible for the operating system to compute how long it is before a page is going to be used, except when all software that will run on a system is either known beforehand and is amendable to the static analysis of its memory reference patterns, or only class of applications allowing run-time analysis is allowed. In spite of this, there exist algorithms which can offer near-optimal performance - on the first run of a program, the operating system keeps track of all the pages which it references, and by using this data, it decides what pages to swap in and out on the second run. This algorithm can offer near-optimal performance, but only on the second run, and only for programs which have been run at least once before, and only if memory reference pattern of program doesn't change significantly between runs.

4.4.4 Not Recently Used

The not recently used (NRU) page replacement algorithm is an algorithm which favours keeping pages which have been recently used. This algorithm works on the following principle: when a page is referenced, a referenced bit will be set for that page, marking it as referenced. Similarly, when a page is modified (written to), a modified bit will be set. The setting of the bits is usually done by the hardware, although it is possible to do so on the software level as well.

At a certain fixedtime interval, the clock interrupt triggers and clears the referenced bit of all the pages, so only pages referenced within the current clock interval are marked with a referenced bit. When a page needs to be replaced, the operating system divides the pages into four categories:

- Category 0: not referenced, not modified
- Category 1: not referenced, modified
- Category 2: referenced, not modified
- Category 3: referenced, modified

Although it does not seem possible for a page to be not referenced yet modified, this happens when a category 3 page has its referenced bit cleared by the clock interrupt. The NRU algorithm simply picks a random page from the lowest category for removal. Note that this algorithm implies that a referenced page is more important than a modified page.

4.4.5 First-In First-Out

The first-in first-out (FIFO) page replacement algorithm is another low-overhead algorithm which requires little bookkeeping on the part of the operating system. The idea is obvious from the name - the operating system keeps track of all the pages in memory in a queue, with the most recent arrival at the back, and the earliest arrival in front. When a page needs to be replaced, the page at the front of the queue is selected, as it will be the oldest page. While FIFO is cheap and intuitive, it performs relatively badly in practical application. Thus, it is rarely used in its unmodified form. This algorithm experiences Belady's anomaly.

4.4.6 Second-Chance

A modified form of the FIFO page replacement algorithm, known as the second chance page replacement algorithm, fares relatively better than FIFO at little cost for the improvement. It works by looking at the front of the queue as FIFO does, but instead of immediately swapping out that page, it checks to see if its referenced bit is set. If it is not set, the page is swapped out. Otherwise, the referenced bit is cleared, and the page is inserted at the back of the queue, as if it were a new page, and this process is repeated. If all the pages have their referenced bit set, on the second encounter of the first page in the list, that page will be swapped out, as it now has its referenced bit cleared.

Essentially, what second-chance does is, as its name suggests, giving every page a "second-chance" - an old page which has been referenced is probably in use, and should not be swapped out over a new page which has not been referenced.

4.4.7 Least Recently Used

The least recently used page (LRU) replacement algorithm, though similar in name to NRU, differs in the fact that LRU keeps track of page usage over a short period of time, while NRU just looks at the usage in the last clock interval. LRU works on the idea that the pages which have been most heavily used in the past few instructions will be used heavily in the next few instructions too. While LRU can provide near-optimal performance in theory, it is rather expensive to implement in practice. There are a few implementation methods for this algorithm which try to reduce the cost yet keep as much of the performance as possible.

The most expensive method is the linked list method, whereby there is a linked list containing all the pages in memory. At the back of this list is the least recently used page, and at the front is the most recently used page. The cost of this implementation lies in the fact that items in the list will have to be moved about every memory reference, which is a very time-consuming process.

Another way, which requires hardware support is as follows: suppose the hardware has a 64-bit counter which is incremented at every instruction. Whenever a page is accessed, it gains a value equal to the counter at the time of page access. Whenever a page needs to be replaced, the operating system simply picks out the page which has the lowest counter, and swaps it out. This is not feasible in present hardware as there exists no such hardware counters.

Because of these implementation costs, one may consider algorithms, such as those which follow, which are similar to LRU, but which offer cheaper implementations.

One important advantage of LRU algorithm is that it is amenable to the full statistical analysis. It has been proved, for example, that LRU can never result in more than N-times more page faults than OPT algorithm, where N is proportional to the number of pages in the managed pool.

On the other hand, LRU weakness is that its performance tends to degenerate under many quite common reference patterns. For example, if there are N pages in the LRU pool, then application doing loop over array of N + 1 pages will cause page fault on each and every access. As loops over large arrays are extremely common a lot of effort was put into modifying LRU to work better in such situations. Many of proposed LRU modifications try to detect looping reference pattern and to switch into suitable replacement algorithm, like Most Recently Used (MRU).

4.4.8 Random

Random replacement algorithm replaces random page in memory. However silly that may sound, this algorithm is useful in certain situations. Usually it fares better than FIFO, and for looping memory references it is better than LRU, although generally LRU performs better in practice.

4.4.9 Not Frequently Used

The not frequently used (NFU) page replacement algorithm also requires a counter, but every page has one counter of its own, which is initially zero. At each clock interval, all pages which have been referenced within that interval will have their counter incremented by 1. In effect, the counters keep track of how frequently a page has been used. Thus, the page with the lowest counter can be swapped out when necessary.

The main problem with NFU is that it keeps track of the frequency of use without regard to the time span of use. Thus, in a multi-pass compiler, pages which were heavily used during the first pass, but are not needed in the second pass will be favoured over pages which are comparably lightly used in the second pass, as they have higher frequency counters. This results in poor performance. Other common scenarios exist where NFU will perform similarly, such as an OS boot-up. Thankfully, a similar and better algorithm exists, and its description follows.

4.4.10 Examples

Examples 1:

A process contains eight virtual pages on disk and is assigned a fixed allocation of four page frames in main memory. The following page trace occurs:

1, 0, 2, 2, 1, 7, 6, 7, 0, 1, 2, 0, 3, 0, 4, 5, 1, 5, 2

Show the successive pages residing in four frames using the LRU and FIFO page replacement policy. Also comment on the effectiveness replacement policy by computing the hit ratio.

Answer

Using LRU Scheme

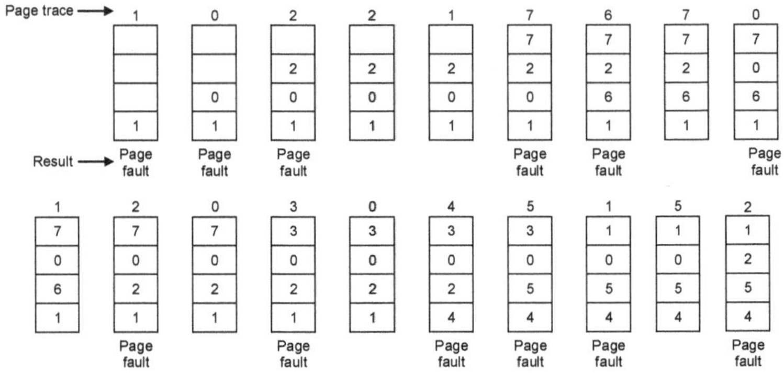

Using FIFO Scheme

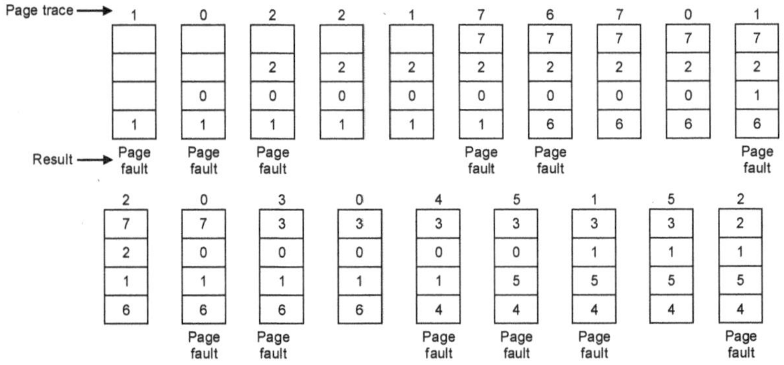

Example 2:

A process contains eight virtual pages on disk and is assigned a fixed allocation of three page frames in main memory. The following page trace occurs:

1 0 2 3 0 1 4 0 1 2 3 4

Show the successive pages residing in three frames using the LRU and Optimal page replacement policy.

Answer

) LRU

Time intervals	1	2	3	4	5	6	7	8	9	10	11	12	Total number of page faults
Reference string	1	0	2	3	0	1	4	0	1	2	3	4	
Frame 1	-	1	0	0	0	0	0	0	0	0	0	3	
Frame 2	-	-	1	1	2	1	1	1	1	1	1	1	
Frame 3	-	-	-	2	3	3	3	4	4	4	2	2	
Page OUT	-	-	-	1	-	2	3	-	-	4	0	1	
Page IN	0	1	2	3	-	1	4	-	-	2	3	4	9

[5]

Optimal

Time intervals	1	2	3	4	5	6	7	8	9	10	11	12	Total number of page faults
Reference string	1	0	2	3	0	1	4	0	1	2	3	4	
Frame 1	-	1	0	0	0	0	0	0	0	0	2	3	
Frame 2	-	-	1	1	1	1	1	1	1	1	1	1	
Frame 3	-	-	-	2	3	3	3	4	4	4	4	4	
Page OUT	-	-	-	2	-	-	3	-	-	0	2	-	
Page IN	0	1	2	3	-	-	4	-	-	2	3	-	7

4.4.11 Thrashing

If the number of frames allocated to a low-priority process falls below the minimum number defined by the computer architecture, the operating system must suspend it's execution by swapping all of its pages, freeing all of its allocated frames.

If a process does not have enough frames, it will very quickly have page fault. At this point, it must replace some page. Since all of its pages are in use, it must replace a page which will be needed again. Consequently, it very quickly faults again and again and so on. This very high paging activity is called thrashing. A process is thrashing if it spends more time for paging than for executing. Thrashing phenomena may cause several performance problems. We explain it in the following example.

The operating system monitors the CPU utilization: if it is low, the degree of multiprogramming is increased by introducing a new process to the system. Suppose a process needs more frames for its execution. It starts to page fault and to take pages from other processes. These processes need those pages, so they also start to fault and to take pages from other processes, and so on. The faulting processes must use the paging device for swapping in and out, so they are queued for the paging device. As result, the ready queue is empty, i.e., the CPU utilization decreases further.

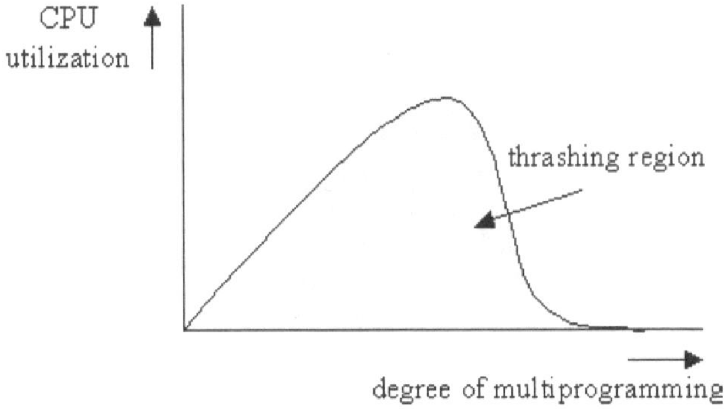

Figure 4.21: Thrashing and its impact on the system performance

The process scheduler finds the decreasing CPU utilization, and increases the degree multiprogramming. The new process tries to take pages from running processes, causing more page faults, and longer queue for the paging device. The CPU utilization drops further, so that the scheduler tries to increase the degree of multiprogramming even more: thrashing occurs and the system "breaks down".

The thrashing effect can be limited by a local replacement scheme. Within the local replacement, if a process starts thrashing, it can not take frames from another process and so cause it to thrash also. Because thrashing processes are in waiting queue for paging device most of the time, the average processing time for a page fault increases. By this way, the effective access time will increase even for processes that are not thrashing.

The thrashing effect can be prevented if a process is allocated as many frames as it needs. The question is how to determine the number of frames a process really needs. One of the possible techniques is the working set strategy, which is looking at what a process is actually using and then deciding how many frames should be allocated. The main goal of this approach is greatly to reduce the page fault rate.

PRACTICE QUESTIONS

Subjective Questions:

Q.1. Describe the paging scheme of memory management with reference to the hardware required to support the system?

Q.2. Consider a paged logical address space (composed of 16 pages of 8 Kbytes each) mapped into a 4 Mbyte physical memory space.

- What is the format of processor's logical address?
- What is the length and width of page table?
- What is the effect on the page table if the physical memory space is reduced by half?

Q.3. A process contains eight virtual pages on disk and is assigned a fixed allocation of four page frames in main memory. The following page trace occurs:

1, 0, 2, 2, 1, 7, 6, 7, 0, 1, 2, 0, 3, 0, 4

Show the successive pages residing in four frames using the LRU and FIFO page replacement policy. Also comment on the effectiveness of replacement policy by computing the hit ratio.

Q.4. What are the major activities of an operating system with respect to memory management?

Q.5. Describe the following allocations algorithm:

i. First Fit

ii. Best Fit

iii. Worst Fit

Q.6. Consider the following segment table.

Segment	Base	Length
0	330	124
1	876	211
2	111	99
3	498	302

On a system using simple segmentation, compute the physical address for each of the following logical addresses. If the address generates a segment fault, indicate so.

(i) 0,99 (ii). 2,78 (iii). 1,265 (iv). 3,222 (v). 0,124

Q.7. Discuss virtual memory management scheme. Compare any two page replacement policies

Q.8. In a paged segment system, a virtual address consists of 32 bits of which 8 bits are displacement, 16 bits are segment number and 8 bits are page number. Calculate the following:

- Page size
- Max Segment size
- Max number of pages
- Max number of Segments

Q.9. One of the design decisions in OS memory management is the choice between swapping and paging. Define each of these terms, and clarify their respective roles in OS memory management.

Q.10. Differentiate between internal and external fragmentation with appropriate example.

Q.11. Consider the virtual page reference string

1, 2, 3, 2, 4, 1, 3, 2, 4, 1

On a demand paged virtual memory system running on a computer system that main memory size of 3 pages frames which are initially empty. Show the successive pages residing in three frames using the LRU and Optimal page replacement policy.

Q.12. What is the purpose of a TLB? Explain the TLB lookup with the help of a block diagram, explaining the hardware required.

Q.13. Consider six memory partitions of size 200 KB, 400 KB, 600 KB, 500 KB, 300 KB, and 250 KB, where KB refers to kilobyte. These partitions need to be allotted to four processes of sizes 357 KB, 210 KB, 468 KB and 491 KB in that order. If the best fit algorithm is used, which partitions are NOT allotted to any process?

Q.14. Consider a paging system with TLB which has 80% hit ratio. It takes 50 nano-seconds time to search the associative registers and 750 nano-seconds time to access memory.

i. Find the time to access a page when the page number is in associative memory.

ii Find the time to access a page when not in associative memory.

iii. Find the effective memory access time.

Q.15. Explain the following memory allocation techniques:

- Fixed partitioning
- Variable partitioning

Supplementary Questions:

Q.1. Prove the belady's anomaly in FIFO page replacement algorithm, assuming that the number of frames is increased from 3 to 4 for the page reference string:-

1,2,3,4,1,2,5,1,2,3,4,5

Assumes all frames are empty initially.

Q.2. Assume a page reference string for a process with m frames (initially all empty). The page reference string has length p with n distinct page numbers occurring in it. For any page-replacement algorithms, what is a lower bound and an upper bound on the number of page faults?

Short Answer Type Questions:

Q.1. What is the main goal of the Memory Management?

Q.2. Under what circumstances worst fit strategy is useful?

Q.3. In a paged system, how is an address viewed?

Q.4. A system uses FIFO policy for page replacement. It has 4 page frames with no pages loaded to begin with. The system first accesses 100 distinct pages in some order and then accesses the same 100 pages but now in the reverse order. How many page faults will occur?

Q.5. What do you mean by logical address?

Q.6. What is a page and what is a frame?

Q.7. What is external fragmentation?

Q.8. Which kind of address is generated by CPU?

Q.9. What is the difference between Swapping and Paging?

Q.10. Increasing the RAM of a computer typically improves performance. Why?

CHAPTER
5

I/O Management and Disk Scheduling

5.1 Disk Input/Output

Computers must manipulate very large quantity of data. Data and programs are stored on high capacity disks and tapes called mass storage media. The most common type of mass storage is made of one or more magnetically coated rigid disks and is called a hard disk drive.

5.1.1 Structure of Hard Disk Drive

A hard disk drive is made of a group of disks, or disk platters stacked on top of one another in an airtight, dust proof case. Each platter has an upper and a lower surface. Each surface has a corresponding read/write head attached to movable arm. The arm between two platters carries two read/write heads.

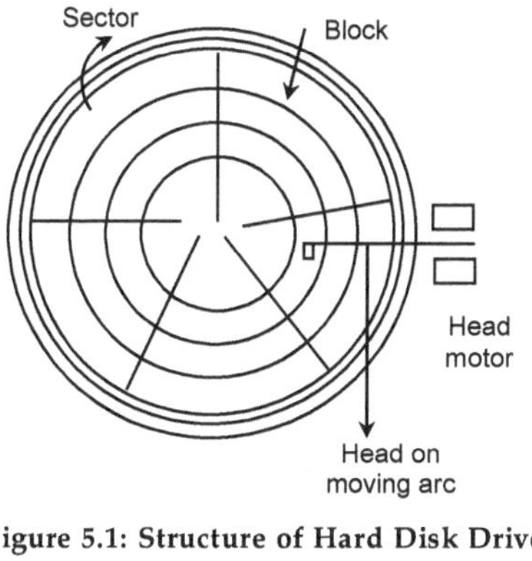

Figure 5.1: Structure of Hard Disk Drive

Tracks and Cylinders: The platter's surface is divided into concentric tracks numbered from the outside, starting with track 0.

Because all read/write heads move simultaneously, it is faster to write on same track of many platters than to fill each platter one after another. The group of tracks having same track number on different platters is called **cylinder**.

Note: A hard disk drive therefore has as many cylinders as it has tracks on one surface of platters.

Sectors: Tracks are divided into sectors. Sectors vary in size. Sectors near center of platter are smaller than sectors near the outer edge but each sector contains the same amount of data. Data density is higher near the center of disk.

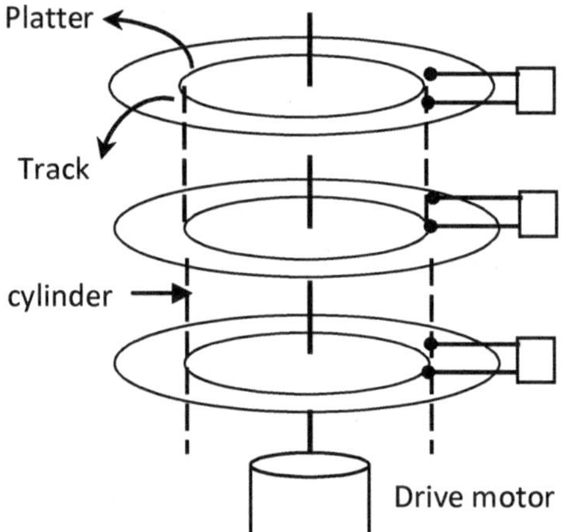

Figure 5.2: Disk Cylenders

Disk Performance Parameters

When the disk drive is operating, the disk is rotating on a constant speed. To read or write, head must be positioned at desired track and at desired sector on that track.

i) **Seek Time:** The time taken in to positioning the head at right track is known as seek time.

ii) **Rotational Delay or Latency Time:** Once the track is selected, the disk controller, waits until the appropriate sector rotates to line up with the head. The time taken for beginning of sector to reach head is known as latency time.

iii) **Access Time:** The sum of seek time and latency time is known as access time.

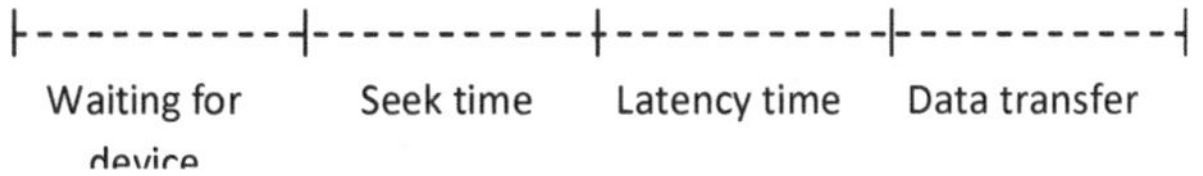

Figure 5.3: Timing of I/O Data Transfer

$$\text{Transfer time} = \frac{b}{rN}$$

b = number of bytes to be transferred

N = Number of bytes on a track

r = rotation speed (revolutions/sec)

5.2 Disk Scheduling Methods

In a typical multiprogramming environment, OS maintains a queue of requests for each I/O devices. So, for a single disk, there will be a number of I/O requests from various processes. If the desired disk drive is available, the request can be serviced immediately otherwise new request is placed on the queue of pending requests for that drive. When the drive becomes available, the I/O request from pending queue is selected by using following policies.

5.2.1 FCFS Scheduling:

This is the simplest form of scheduling, which simply means that we process items from the queue in sequential order.

Consider, for example, a disk queue with request for I/O to blocks on cylinders: 98, 183, 37, 122, 14, 124, 65, 67. Disk head is initially at cylinder 53.

The schedule is shown below:

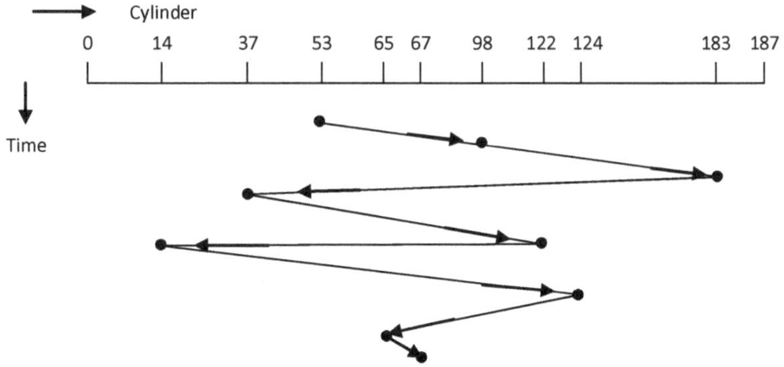

Advantage: This strategy has the advantage of being fair because request is honored in the order received.

Disadvantage: It does not provide the fast service. In the previous example, the wild swing from 122 to 14 and then back to 124 illustrate the problem with this schedule.

In the example, total head movement is of 640 cylinders which can be reduced by following policy.

5.2.2 Shortest Seek Time First (SSTF)

This policy selects the disk I/O request that requires the least movement of disk arm from current position. Since the seek time increases with number of cylinders traversed by the head, SSTF chooses the pending request closest to current head position.

So the scheduling for previous example,

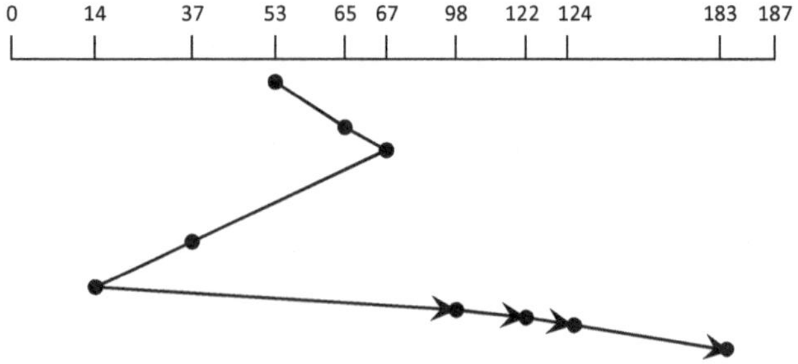

Advantage: This policy results in minimal head movement and thus, seek length is minimal. In example total head movement is of 236 cylinders.

Disadvantage

Starvation: If there is a consistent supply of I/O request closer to head position, I/O requests of cylinders for from head will never be serviced.

5.2.3 Elevator Algorithm - Scan Scheduling

In the scan algorithm disk arm starts at one end of disk, and moves towards the other end, servicing requests as it reaches each cylinder, until it gets to the other end of disk. At the other end, direction of head movement is reversed and servicing continues.

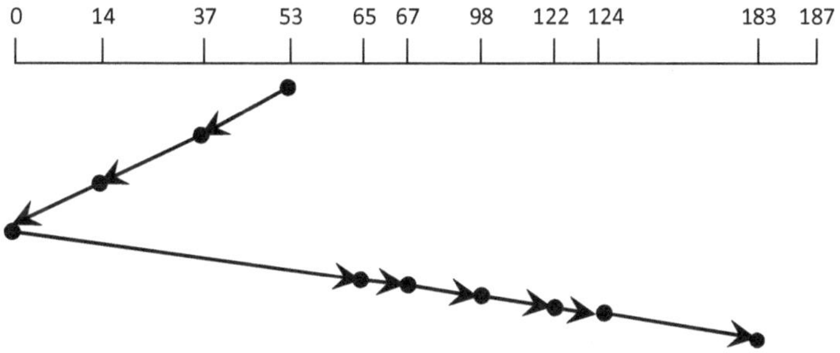

Advantage: If the request arrives in queue just in front of head, it will be serviced almost immediately.

Disadvantage: If request arrives just behind head, it will have to wait until arm moves to the end of disk, reverses direction and comes back.

When disk arm reaches to an end and reverses the direction, the heaviest density of request will be at other end of disk.

5.2.4 C-Scan Scheduling

Like the scan scheduling, in C–Scan, head moves from one end to another end of disk, servicing the request along the way but when it reaches to an end it immediately returns to the beginning of disk.

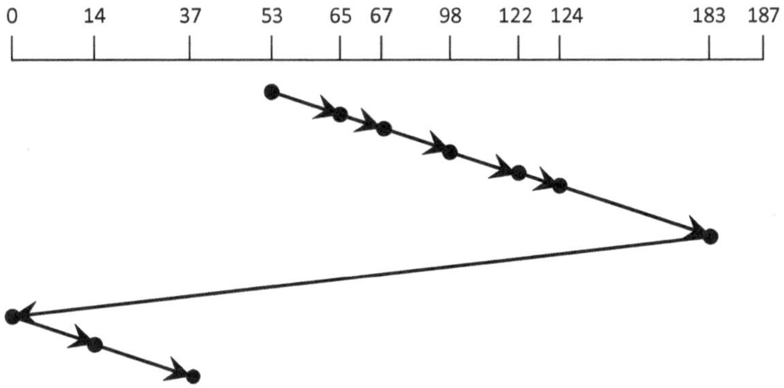

Look Scheduling

Unlike the Scan and C-Scan (the arm moves across the full width of disk), in Look scheduling arm goes only as far as the final request in each direction.

Like the Scan and C-Scan, it also has version C-Look.

5.3 Disk Management

The operating system is responsible for several other aspects of disk manage-ment, too. Here we discuss disk initialization, booting from disk, and bad-block recovery.

5.3.1 Disk Formatting

A new magnetic disk is a blank slate: It is just platters of a magnetic recording material. Before a disk cart store data, it must be divided into sectors that the disk controller can read and write. This process is called low-level formatting (or physical formatting). Low-level formatting fills the disk with a special data structure for each sector The data structure for a sector typically consists of a header, a data area (usually 512 bytes in size), and a trailer. The header and trailer contain information used by the disk controller, such as a sector number and an error-correcting code (ECC). When the controller writes a sector of data during normal I/O, the ECC is updated with a value calculated from all the bytes in the data area. When the sector is read, the ECC is recalculated and is compared with the stored value. If the stored a nil calculated numbers are different, this mismatch indicates that the data area of the sector has become corrupted and that the disk sector may be bad. The ECC is an error-correcting code because it contains enough information that, if only a few bits of data have been corrupted, the controller can identify which bits have changed and can calculate what their correct values should be. The controller automatically does the ECC processing whenever a sector is read or written.

Most hard disks are low-level formatted at the factory as a part of the manufacturing process. This formatting enables the manufacturer to test the disk and to initialize the mapping from logical block numbers to defect-free sectors on the disk. For many hard disks, when the disk controller is instructed to low-level format the disk, it can also be told how many bytes of data space to leave between the header and trailer of all sectors It is usually possible to choose among a few sizes, such as 256, 512, and 1,024 bytes. Formatting a disk with a larger sector size means that fewer sectors can fit on each track, but that also means fewer headers and trailers are written on each track, and thus increases the space available for user data. Some operating systems can handle only a sector size of 512 bytes.

To use a disk to hold files, the operating system still needs to record its own data structures on the disk. It does so in two steps. The first step is to partition the disk into one or more groups of cylinders. The operating system can treat each partition as though it were a separate disk. For instance, one partition can hold a copy of the operating system's executable code, while another holds user files. After partitioning, the second step is logical formatting (or creation of a file system). In this step, the operating system stores the initial file-system data structures onto the disk. These data structures may include maps of free and allocated space (a FAT or inodes) and an initial empty directory.

Some operating systems give special programs the ability to use a disk partition as a large sequential array of logical blocks, without any file-system data structures. This array is sometimes called the raw disk, and I/O to this may is termed raw I/O. For example, some database systems prefer raw I/O because it enables them to control the exact disk location where each database record is stored. Raw I/O bypasses all the file-system services, such as the buffer cache, file locking, prefetching, space allocation, file names, and directories. We can make certain applications more efficient by implementing their own special-purpose storage services on a raw partition, but most applications perform better when they use the regular file-system services.

5.3.2 Boot Block

For a computer to start running – for instance, when it is powered up or rebooted – it needs to have an initial program to run. This initial bootstrap program tends to be simple. It initializes all aspects of the system, from CPU registers to device controllers and the contents of main memory, and then starts the operating system. To do its job, the bootstrap program finds the operating-system kernel on disk, loads that kernel into memory, and jumps to an initial address to begin the operating-system execution.

For most computers, the bootstrap is stored in read-only memory (ROM) This location is convenient, because ROM needs no initialization and is at a fixed location that the processor can start executing when powered up or reset. And, since ROM is read only, it cannot be infected by a computer virus. The problem is that changing this bootstrap code requires changing the ROM hardware chips. For this reason, most systems store a tiny bootstrap loader program in the boot ROM, whose only job is to bring in a full bootstrap program from disk. The full bootstrap program can be changed easily: A new version is simply written onto the disk. The full bootstrap program is stored in a partition called the boot blocks, at a fixed location on the disk. A disk that has a boot partition is called a boot disk or system disk.

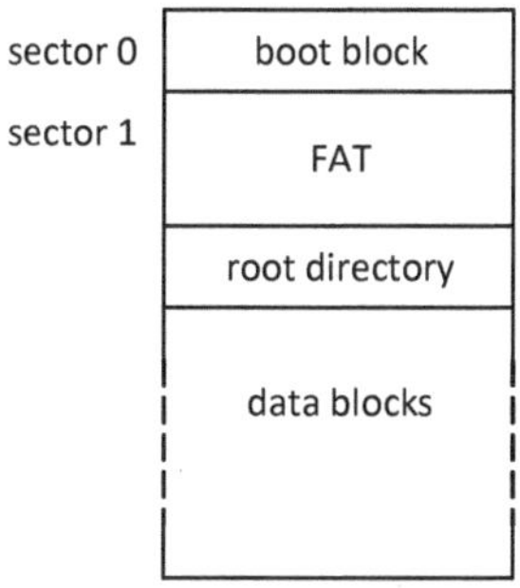

Figure 5.4: MS-DOS Disk Layout

The code in the boot ROM instructs the disk controller to read the boot blocks into memory (no device drivers are loaded at this point), and then starts executing that code. The full bootstrap program is more sophisticated than the bootstrap loader in the boot ROM; it is able to load the entire operating system from a non-fixed location on disk, and to start the operating system running. Even so, the full bootstrap code may be small. For example, MS-DOS uses one 512-byte block for its boot program.

5.3.3 Bad Blocks

Because disks have moving parts and small tolerances (recall that the disk head flies just above the disk surface), they are prone to failure. Sometimes the failure is complete, and the disk needs to be replaced, and its contents restored from backup media to the new disk. More frequently, one or more sectors become defective. Most disks even come from the factory with bad blocks. Depending on the disk and controller in use, these blocks are handled in a variety of ways.

On simple disks, such as some disks with IDE controllers, bad blocks are handled manually. For instance, the MS-DOS format command does a logical format and, as a part of the process, scans the disk to find bad blocks. If format finds a bad block, it writes a special value into the corresponding FAT entry to tell the allocation routines not to use that block. If blocks go bad during normal operation, a special program (such as chkdsk) must be run manually to search for the bad blocks and to lock them away as before. Data that resided on the bad blocks usually are lost.

More sophisticated disks, such as the SCSI disks used in high-end PCs and most workstations and servers, are smarter about bad-block recovery. The controller maintains a list of bad blocks on the disk. The list is initialized during the low-level format at the factory, and is updated over the life of the disk. Low-level formatting also sets aside spare sectors not visible to the operating system. The controller can be told to replace each bad sector logically with one of the spare sectors. This scheme is known as sector sparing or forwarding.

A typical bad-sector transaction might be as follows;

i) The operating system tries to read logical block 87.

ii) The controller calculates the ECC and finds that the sector is bad. It reports this finding to the operating system.

iii) The next time that the system is rebooted, a special command is run to tell the SCSI controller to replace the bad sector with a spare.

iv) After that, whenever the system requests logical block 87, the request is translated into the replacement sector's address by the controller.

Such a redirection by the controller could invalidate any optimization by the operating system's disk-scheduling algorithm! For this reason, most disks ire formatted to provide a few spare sectors in each cylinder, and a spare cylinder as well. When a bad block is remapped, the controller uses a spare sector from the same cylinder, if possible.

As an alternative to sector sparing, some controllers can be instructed to replace a bad block by sector slipping. Here is an example: Suppose that logical block 17 becomes defective, and the first available spare follows sector 202. Then, sector slipping would remap all the sectors from 17 to 202, moving them all down one spot. That is, sector 202 would be copied into the spare, then sector 201 into 202, and then 200 into 201, and so on, until sector 18 is copied into sector 19. Slipping the sectors in this way frees up the space of sector 18, so sector 17 can be mapped to it.

The replacement of a bad block generally is not a totally automatic process because the data in the bad block are usually lost. Thus, whatever file was using that block must be repaired (for instance, by restoration from a backup tape), and that requires manual intervention.

5.4 Swap-Space Management

Swap-space management is another low-level task of the operating system. Virtual memory uses disk space as an extension of main memory. Since disk access is much slower than memory access, using swap space significantly decreases system performance. The main goal for the design and implemen-tation of swap space is to provide the best throughput for the virtual-memory system, in this section, we discuss how swap space is used, where swap space is located on disk, and how swap space is managed.

5.4.1 Swap-Space Use

Swap space is used in various ways by different operating systems, depending on the implemented memory-management algorithms. For instance, systems that implement swapping may use swap space to hold the entire process image, including the code and data segments. Paging systems may simply store pages that have been pushed out of main memory. The amount of swap space needed on a system can therefore vary depending on the amount of physical memory. The amount of virtual memory it is backing, and the way in which the virtual memory is used. It can range from a few megabytes of disk space to gigabytes.

Some operating systems, such as UNIX, allow the use of multiple swap spaces. These swap spaces are usually put on separate disks, so the load placed on the I/O system by paging and swapping can be spread over the system's I/O devices.

Note that it is safer to overestimate than to underestimate swap space, because if a system runs out of swap space it may be forced to abort processes or may crash entirely. Overestimation wastes disk space that could otherwise be used for files, but does no other harm.

5.4.2 Swap-Space Location

A swap space can reside in two places: Swap space can be carved out of the normal file system, or it can be in a separate disk partition. If the swap space is simply a large file within the file system, normal file-system routines can be used to create it, name it, and allocate its space. This approach, though easy to implement, is also inefficient. Navigating the directory structure and the disk-allocation data structures takes time and (potentially) extra disk accesses. External fragmentation can greatly increase swapping times by forcing multiple seeks during reading or writing of a process image. We can improve perfor-mance by caching the block location information in physical memory, and by using special tools to allocate physically contiguous blocks for the swap file, but the cost of traversing the file-system data structures still remains.

Alternatively, swap space can be created in a separate disk partition. No file system or directory structure is placed on this space. Rather, a separate swap-space storage manager is used to allocate and deallocate the blocks. This manager uses algorithms optimized for speed, rather than for storage efficiency. Internal fragmentation may increase, but this tradeoff is acceptable because data in the swap space generally live for much shorter amounts of time than do files in the file system, and the swap area may be accessed much more frequently. This approach creates a fixed amount of swap space during disk partitioning. Adding more swap space can be done only via repartitioning of the disk (which involves moving or destroying and restoring the other file-system partitions from backup), or via adding another swap space elsewhere.

5.4.3 Performance Issues

As with any component of the operating system, the three most important aspens of tertiary-storage performance are speed, reliability, and cost.

Speed

The speed of tertiary storage has two aspects: bandwidth and latency. \ft measure the bandwidth in bytes per second. The sustained bandwidth is the average data rate during a large transfer, that is, the number of bytes divided by the transfer time. The effective bandwidth calculates the average over the entire I/O time, including the time for seek or locate and any cartridge-switching time in a jukebox. In essence, the sustained bandwidth is the data rate when the data stream is actually flowing, and the effective bandwidth it the overall data rate provided by the drive. The bandwidth of a drive is generally understood to mean the sustained bandwidth.

For removable disks, the bandwidth ranges from less than 0.25 MB per second for the slowest, to several megabytes per second for the fastest. Tapes have an even wider range of bandwidths, from less than 0.25 MB per second to over 30 MB per second. The fastest tape drives have significantly higher bandwidth than do removable disk drives.

The second aspect of speed is the access latency. By this performance measure, disks are much faster than tapes: Disk storage is essentially two-dimensional – all the bits are out in the open. A disk access simply moves the arm to the selected cylinder and waits for the rotational latency, which may tab less than 5 milliseconds. By contrast, tape storage is three-dimensional. At aw time, a small portion of the tape is accessible to the head, whereas most of the bits are buried below hundreds or thousands of layers of tape wound on the reel. A random access on tape requires winding the tape reels until the selected block reaches the tape head, which can take tens or hundreds of seconds. Sc we can generally say that random access within a tape cartridge is more than a thousand times slower than random access on disk.

If a jukebox is involved, the access latency can be significantly higher. For a removable disk to be changed, the drive must stop spinning, then the robotic arm must switch the disk cartridges, and the drive must spin up the new cartridge. This operation takes several seconds – about a hundred times large than the random-access time within one disk. So switching disks in a jukebox incurs a relatively high performance penalty.

For tapes, the robotic-arm time is about the same as for disk. But for tape to be switched, the old tape generally must rewind before it can be ejected, an; that operation can take as long as 4 minutes And, after a new tape is load into the drive, many seconds can be required for the drive to calibrate itself to the tape and to prepare for I/O. Although a slow tape jukebox can have a tape switch time of 1 or 2 minutes, this time is not enormously larger than the random-access time within one tape.

So, to generalize, we say that random access in a disk jukebox has a latency a tens of seconds, whereas random access in a tape jukebox has a latency of hundreds of seconds; switching disks is expensive, but switching tapes is not. Be careful not to over-generalize: Some expensive tape jukeboxes can rewind, eject load a new tape, and fast forward to a random item of data all in less than 30 seconds.

5.5 File System Interface and Implementation

5.5.1 Introduction

It becomes essential to store information for long-term so that it can be accessed at any time. As seen in earlier chapters, it is also essential to make data sharable among various processes. Also that this information can be **huge in size** and therefore, must be accommodated on the appropriate storage devices. Thus, these are three essential requirements for long-term information storage. It indicates that information should be stored on disks and other external media in units called files. Processes, running in the system can read or write these storage media via files. Information stored in files must be persistent, i.e., it should not be affected by process creation and termination.

Files are managed by the operating system. How are they structured, named, accessed, protected and implemented are few major considerations in operating system design. The part of operating system, which deals with files, is known as the file system.

File Concepts

Physically, a file is the smallest allotment of secondary storage device for example disks. Logically a file is sequence of logical records, i.e., a sequence of bits and bytes. A file has various attributes like name, type, location, size, protection, time and data of creation, user information etc. Let us look at various attributes from the user's point of view.

File Attributes

A file has a name and data. Other than this, the operating system can associate other information like date and time of file creation, file's current size etc. with a file. These are known as attributes of a file. Following shows a list of possible attributes. The list of these attributes varies from system to system.

Table 10.2: Some Possible File Attributes

Field	Meaning
Protection	Who can access the file and in what way
Password	Password needed to access the file
Creator	Id of person who created the file
Owner	Current owner
Read only flag	0 for read/write, 1 for read only
Hidden flag	0 for normal. 1 for do not display in listings
System flag	0 for normal file, 1 for system file
Archive flag	0 has been backed up, 1 for needs to be backed up
ASCII/binary flag	0 for ASCII file. 1 for binary file
Random access flag	0 for sequential access only. 1 for random access
Record length	Number of bytes in a record
Key position	Offset of the key within each record
Key length	Number of bytes in the key field
Creation time	Date and time file was created
Time of last access	Date and time file was last accessed
Time of last change	Date and time file was last changed
Current size	Number of bytes in the file
Maximum size	Maximum size file may grow to

File Preparation

Files exist to store information and allow it to be retrieved later. Different systems provide different operations to allow storage and retrieval. The following list shows the most common file operations available via system calls:

1) **Create:** A blank file is created. The purpose of this call is to create a new blank file with the specified attributes.

2) **Delete:** The purpose of this system call is to delete this file from the disk when it is not needed.

3) **Open:** Before using a file either for reading or writing, it must be opened. The purpose of this call is to allow the system to fetch the attributes and list of disk addresses into main memory for rapid access on subsequent calls. This is a very important concept, which relates to caching.

4) **Close:** When a file is no longer accessed, it must be closed using this system call

5) **Read:** When a file is only to be read, this call is used. The location of the data to be read must be specified. The size of data to be read must also be specified.

6) **Write:** Data can be written to file with this system call. The data is written at the current position in the file and if the current position is at the end of the file, then the file size increases automatically.

7) **Append:** This call is a restricted form of WRITE. It can only add data to the end of the file.

8) **Seek:** This call is used to reposition the current pointer to a specific place in the file. After this call succeeds the pointer is placed at the desired location and data is read or written there, using another system call (like READ or WRITE).

9) **Get Attributes:** Processes often need to know the attributes of some files to do their work. For example, a process might want to display the id of the person who created the file. Therefore, it can use this system call to get the attributes of that file.

10) **Set Attributes:** Using this system call, attributes of a file can be set. For example, a user may want to set its read-only flag to 1, so that it can only be read by the users and thus, cannot be written.

11) **Rename:** A user may need to change the name of a file very often. Therefore, this functionality is provided by RENAME system call.

Protection, password, creator and owner attributes are basically used to protect a file from unauthorized access. Some systems provide the privilege to lock a file with some particular password. Only those users who know this password can then access this file. The flags mentioned in above table, are used to enable or disable some specific property of a file. A file can be made read-only, hidden, system-file, and so-on by setting its read only flag to 1, its hidden flag to 1, its system flag to 1 and so on. The archive flag is a bit that keeps track of whether the file has been backed up or not? Once the backup of a file has been taken, its backup bit is set to 0. Operating system sets this bit to 1 whenever a change takes place in the contents of this file, so that it should again be backed up the user, using a back up program. Record length, key position and key length fields are only present in files whose records can be searched using a key.

The various time attributes keep track of when the file was created, most recently accessed and most recently modified. This information may be necessary to know that if the source file has been modified after the creation of the corresponding object file, then it needs to be compiled again. Maximum size attribute is used by some systems, which require the maximum size to be specified when the file is created.

5.5.2 File Access Methods

Files can be categorized broadly into two types depending upon their access methods. Sequential files are those, which are read sequentially (one record, then another and so on) in an order, starting at the beginning to the end of the file. Sequential files can be rewound so that they can be read as often as needed. However, records in such files cannot be read out of order for example, reading of 34th record followed by 5th record and then 1st record is not possible with sequential files Sequential files are convenient when the storage media is serial-access, for example, magnetic tape rather than direct-access, for example, magnetic disk.

Files whose records can be read in any order are called random access files. Random access files are basically a collection of records stored on a disk and these records are numbered 1, 2, 3 and so on and therefore, can be referred to by their numbers instead of their position. Such files should be necessarily be stored on direct access media like disk.

Random access files are essential for many applications, for example, data base systems. In a banking application, a customer may want to look up his current balance. This can be easily done by locating this customer's record using his account number as a key, rather than sequentially reading the records for thousands of other customers before this customer's record is located and read.

It is worth mentioning here that not all operating systems support both sequential and random access for files. Some systems allow only sequential file access, others allow only random access. Some systems require that a file should be defined as sequential or random when it is created, so that it can be accessed in the way it has been declared.

5.6 Directory Structure

To keep track of files, the file systems normally provide directories, which, in many systems, are themselves treated as files. A directory contains information about files. Thus, it is central to the functioning of the file system. A directory is used as a means to group the files owned by a user. This notion of grouping can be extended to permit grouping of files according to some user-defined criteria. This section focuses upon directories, their properties, organization and the operations that can be performed on them.

5.6.1 Hierarchical Directory Systems

A directory typically contains a number of entries, one per file. One possibility is that each entry contains the file name, the file attributes, and the disk address where the file is stored. Another possibility is that a directory entry holds the file name and a pointer to another data structure where the attributes and disk addresses are found. Both of these systems are commonly used. Following Figure depicts the two ways to represent a directory.

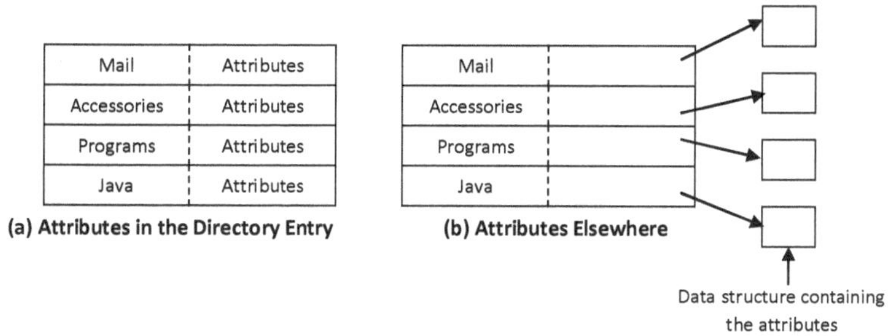

Figure 5.5: Directories

When a file is opened, the operating system searches the directory structure until it finds the name of the file to be opened. It then extracts the attributes and disk addresses, either directly from the directory entry or from the data structure pointed to, and puts them in a table in main memory. All subsequent references to the file use the information that has been fetched in the main memory.

The number of directories varies from system to system. The simple design is for the system to maintain a single directory containing all the files of all the users, as illustrated in following figure. In this case, however, if there are many users, and they choose the same file names, conflicts and confusion will make the system unworkable. This system model is used only by the most primitive operating systems.

An improvement on the idea of having a single directory for all files to have one directory per user as shown in figure (b). This design eliminates name conflicts among users, but is not very satisfactory for users with many files. It is quite common for users to want to group their files together in logical ways. For example, I may wish to have a collection of the files related to operating system concepts) to be consulted by me while writing this book). Similarly, I may wish to have a collection of files containing assignments submitted by my students learning Java or a collection of files containing the source code of my project work etc.

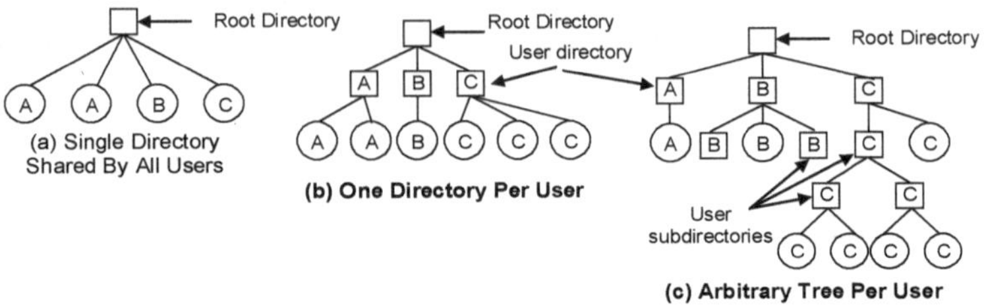

Figure 5.6: Three File System Designs. The Letters Indicate Name or Files Or Directories

A general hierarchy (i.e., a tree of directories) is thus needed. With this approach, each user can have as many directories as are needed so that files can be grouped together in natural ways. This approach is shown in **figure (c)**. Here the directories A, B, and C contained in the root directory each belong to a different user and two (B and C) of them have subdirectories for two different projects.

5.6.2 Directory Operations

Many systems calls are allowed for managing directories. They vary from system to system. This part of text discusses some common system calls used to manipulate directories.

1) **Create:** A directory is created. It is empty except for dot (•) and dotdot (••), which are put there automatically by the system.
2) **Delete:** A directory is deleted. Only an empty directory can be deleted. A directory containing only dot and dotdot is considered empty, as these usually cannot be deleted. In order to delete a directory having subdirectories, first the subdirectories should be deleted.
3) **Opendir:** Directories can be opened for reading it. For example, to list all the files in a directory, a listing program opens the directory to read out the names of all the files it contains. Before a directory can be read, it must be opened.
4) **Closedir:** When a directory has been read, it should be closed to free up internal table space in main memory.

5) **Readdir:** This call returns the next entry in an open director)' Formerly, it was possible to read directories using the usual READ system call, but that approach has the disadvantage of forcing the programmer to know and deal with the internal structure of directories. In contrast, READDIR always returns one entry in a standard format, no matter which of the possible directory structures are being used.

6) **Rename:** Directories can be renamed just like files.

7) **Link:** This system call specifies an existing file and a path name, and creates a link from the existing file to the name specified by the path. In this way, the same file may appear in multiple directories.

8) **Unlink:** A directory entry is removed. If the File being unlinked is present only in one directory, it is removed from the file system. If it is present in multiple directories, only the path name specified is removed and the others remain as such.

5.7 File Protection

File systems often contain information that is highly valuable to their users. Protecting this information against unauthorized usage is therefore, a major concern of alt the file systems. In the following sub-sections we will look at a variety of issues concerned with file protection.

5.7.1 Access Control

The access to a particular file can be controlled by limiting the types of file access that can be made. Following are the few file operations that can be controlled:

Read	Read a file
Write	Write the file
Append	Append a file
Delete	Delete a file
List	List the name and attributes of a file
Rename	Rename a file
Edit	Changing the contents of a file
Copy	Make a copy of a file.

One way to control these operations in through access control lists (ACLs) and groups. An access list may be associated with each file and directory. This list may contain the user name and the types of access allowed for each user. The operating system checks this access control list (associated with a file) whenever a user requests an access to a particular file. If that user is listed for the requested access, the access is allowed. Otherwise, user is denied access to the file.

The main problem with access controls list (ACLs) is their length. If we want to allow every-one to read a file, we must list all users with read access. To overcome this problem many systems classify the users of a file into three types:

i) **Owner:** The user who created the file.

ii) **Group:** A set of users who are sharing the file and need similar access.

iii) **Universe:** All remaining users in the system constitute universe.

Thus, if a person has created a file, he/she is owner of the file, [f the owner has given execute-only permission (on his file) to some set of users, then this set of users constitute a group and all users in this group have execute-only permission for the file. All the other possible users will fall into the universe category and probably may be given read-only access to the file. UNIX operating system uses this method to provide protection to the files. Access control lists should be created and maintained by some administrator, file owner or any other manager of the organization.

5.7.2 Other Protection Mechanisms

Files can be protected by a password. The owner of a file can control its access by assigning a password. Thus, only those users who know the password, can access a particular file.

Disadvantages of this scheme are:

i) If a separate password is associated with each file, the user will have to remember so many passwords and the scheme will become impractical.

ii) If only one password is used for protecting all files, then cracking of one password by an unauthorized user will enable him to access all the files.

This problem can be dealt by associating a password with a subdirectory rather than with an individual file.

5.8 File System Organization

So far, we have discussed the users' view of a file system. Let us now look at implementers view. Users are concerned with how files are named, what operations are allowed on them, what the directory tree looks like, and similar interface issues. Implementers are interested in how files and directories are stored, how disk space is managed, and how to make everything work efficiently and reliably. Let us examine the file implementation issues here.

The key issue in implementing file storage is keeping track of which disk blocks go with which file. Various methods are used in different systems.

5.8.1 Contiguous Allocation

The simplest allocation scheme is to store each file as a contiguous block of data on the disk. Thus, on a disk having blocks size 1k, a 25k file would be allocated 25 consecutive blocks. This scheme has two significant advantages:

i) It is simple to implement because keeping a track of where a file's blocks are, is reduced to remembering one number only. This number is the disk address of the first block occupied by the file.

ii) Performance is good because entire file can be read from (he disk in a single operation (just because it is stored contiguously).

Disadvantages of this scheme are:

i) It is not feasible unless the maximum file size is known at the time of file creation. If it is not known, the operating system does not know how much disk space should be reserved.

ii) Fragmentation of the disk may occur as a result of this scheme. Therefore, space is wasted that might otherwise have been used. Compaction cannot be applied as a solution to this problem, because compaction of the disk is expensive.

5.8.2 Linked List Allocation

The second method for storing files is to keep each one as a linked list of disk blocks, as shown in following figure. The first word of each block is used as a pointer to the next one. The rest of the block is used for storing data.

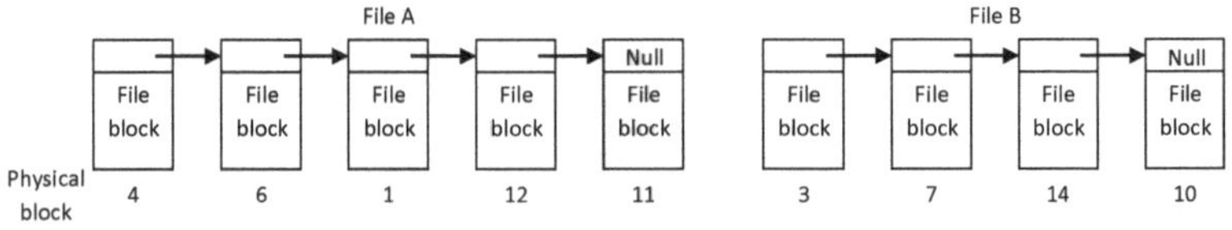

Figure 5.7: Storing a File as a Linked List of Disk Blocks

Advantages of this scheme are:

i) Unlike contiguous allocation, every disk block can be utilized by this method. Thus' there is least possibility of disk fragmentation.

ii) The directory entry can merely store the disk address of the first block and this can -\ be used to find the rest of the blocks occupied by the file.

This scheme however, suffers from the following disadvantages:

i) Although reading a file sequentially is easy, but random access becomes extremely slow.

ii) Pointer takes up space in each disk block and therefore, the amount of data storage in a block is no longer a power of two, which otherwise would have been a power of two. This is essential because most programs read and write data in blocks whose size is a power of two.

5.8.3 Linked List Allocation Using an Index

This scheme is an attempt to remove the disadvantages of the linked list allocation. Here, instead of having a pointer, an index is maintained. For the above figure, where the linked allocation of two files namely A and B has been shown, table or index like the one shown in following figure can be used. Using the table of following figure, for file A we can start with the block 4 and follow the linked list all the way to the end. The same way for file B, we can start from block 3 and follow the linked list.

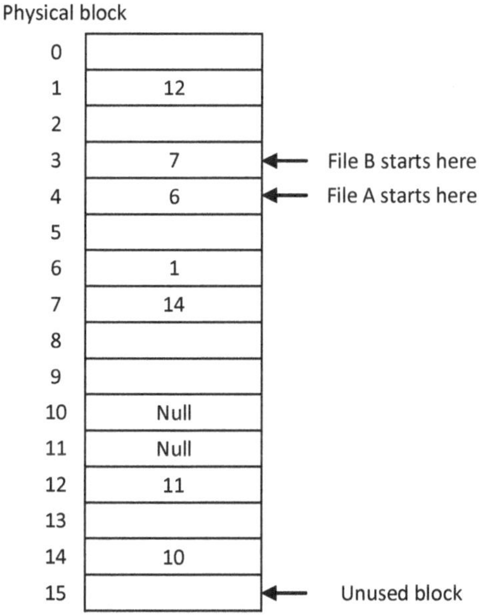

Figure 5.8: Linked List Allocation Using a Table in Main Memory

Advantages of this scheme are:

i) The entire block is available for data. No space is consumed by pointers etc.

ii) Random access is easier. This is so because, no doubt, the chain has to be followed to locate a particular part of a file, but because the index is in memory, the seek operations do not involve disk references as in the previous case.

iii) Here also, the directory entry can merely store the disk address of the first block and this can be used to find the rest of the blocks occupied by the file. This method is used by MS-DOS for disk allocation.

Disadvantages of this scheme are:

i) The entire index or table will have to be kept in main memory for all the time to make it work. This may prove to be hazardous if the disk is large and thus the table or index is also large.

ii) Looking up for an entry in such a large index will also become very time consuming.

5.8.4 I-nodes

This method for keeping track of which block belongs to which file, is used by UNIX operating system. In this scheme, each file is associated with a little table called an i-node (index node), which lists the attributes and disk addresses of the file's blocks. I-nodes are shown in following figure.

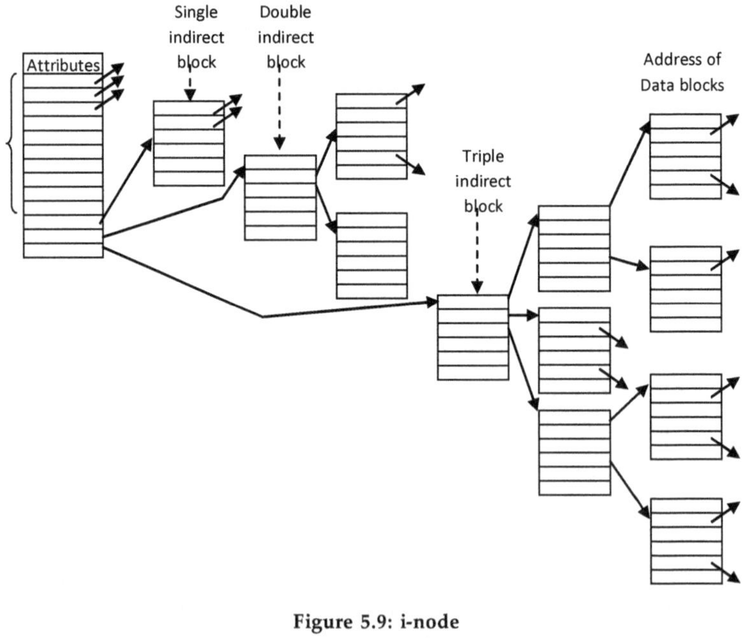

Figure 5.9: i-node

This scheme is implemented as follows:

i) For small files, the first few disk addresses and all the necessary information are stored in the i-node itself. Whenever a file is opened, all this information is fetched from disk to main memory.

ii) For somewhat larger file, one of the addresses in the i-node is the address of a disk block called single indirect block. This block contains additional disk addresses.

iii) For even more large file, the i-node may contain another address which is the address of a disk block called a double indirect block. This J>lock contains the addresses of the blocks containing the lists of single indirect blocks. Each of these single indirect blocks point to a few hundred data blocks. Similarly, a triple indirect block can also be used.

5.9 Free Space Management

It becomes necessary to reuse the disk space created after deleting the files so that new files can use it. The operating system maintains a free-space list to keep track of free disk space. Whenever, a new file is created, the free-space list is searched for the required amount of space. This free space is allocated to the newly created file and its entry is then removed from the free-space list. When a file is deleted, the disk space freed up by it is then added to the free-space list.

Let us now understand the various possible methods of implementing free-space list:

5.9.1 Bit Map

The free space list is implemented as a bit map. Every bit represents a block on the disk. The bit for a block is I if it is free and u is 0 if the block is allocated. This bit map is stored on specific place on the disk. The free-space bit map is as shown in following figure.

Blocks	0	1	2	3	4	5	6	7	8	9	10	11	12	13
Bits	0	0	1	1	1	1	0	0	1	1	1	1	0	0

Figure 5.10: Bit Map

The above figure indicates that the blocks 2, 3, 4, 5, 8, 9, 10, 11 are free and rest of the blocks are allocated.

Advantages of this approach are:

It is simple and efficient to find the first free block or n consecutive free blocks on the disk. To find the first free block, the operating system checks sequentially each word in the bit map to see whether that value is not 0. The first non-0 word is scanned for the first 1 bit, which is the location of the first free block.

Disadvantages of this approach are:

i) This may require special hardware support (bit operation) to find the first T in a word if it is not zero.

ii) Bit maps are inefficient unless they are kept in main memory and are written to disk occasionally for recovery needs. If the disk size is large, the corresponding bit map is large and thus keeping it in the main memory is not possible. Consider that the disk size is 1 GB Þ 2^{30} bytes and the block size is 2^{12} bytes then the number of blocks will be $2^{30}/2^{12} = 2^{18}$ and corresponding to each block, a bit will be there in the bit map. This implies that size of bit map will be 2^{18} bits = 256 KB.

5.9.2 Linked List

This approach maintains a linked list of all the free disk blocks. The first free block in the list can be pointed out by a head pointer, which is kept in a special location on the disk following figure shows the linked list of free blocks represented by bit map shown in above figure.

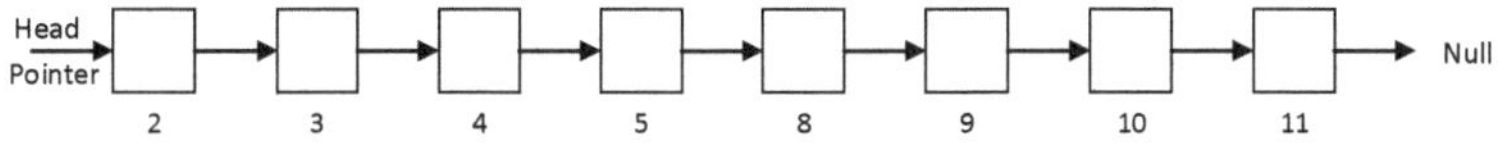

Figure 5.11: Linked Free Space List on Disk

Advantages of this approach are:

Whenever a file is to be allocated a free block, the operating system can simply allocate the first block in the free space-list and move the head pointer to the next free block in the list.

Disadvantages of this approach are:

i) Traversing the free space list will be very time consuming; each block will have to be read from the disk, which is read very slowly as compared to the main memory.

ii) Pointers used in the linked list will consume disk space.

5.9.3 Grouping

Another approach is to store the addresses of n free blocks in the first free block. The last block contains the addresses of another n free blocks and so on. This means that first n-2 blocks of these blocks arc actually free (as the first and last blocks of the group will contain addresses). The advantage of this approach over linked list approach is that by accessing only one block, the addresses of a large number of free blocks can be known at once.

5.9.4 Counting

Another approach takes into consideration that generally, several contiguous blocks may be allocated or freed simultaneously, particularly when contiguous allocation algorithm has been used for allocating disk space. Thus, instead of keeping a list of addresses of n free blocks, it is more convenient to keep the address of the first free blocks and the number n of free contiguous blocks that follow the first block. Therefore, each entry in the free space list then consists of a disk address and a count. This may make the overall list shorter in size.

5.10 Protection and Security

5.10.1 Why Protection?

The various processes (user and system processes) must be protected from one other's activities. Protection mechanisms deal with controlling the access of programs, processes or users to the resources of a computer system. Security, which is discussed later, is however, an issue that requires a control over the external environment within which the system operates. Internal protection is of no use if the computer system is accessed by an unauthorized individual who can remove some important files or insert a virus into the system and make it non-functional.

5.10.2 Goals of Protection

The protection mechanism to be enforced into a system should have the following goals:

i) In multi-programming systems, the operating system should enable the users to safely share a common logical address space such as files etc. It should also enable the users to share a common physical address space, i.e., memory. In such systems, therefore, the goal should be to prevent accidental and intentional destructive behavior.

ii) Ensure fair and reliable resource usage, i.e., each program component active in a system should use the system resources only in accordance with certain policies (stated for the use of these resources). Since the policies for a resource usage may vary, dependency upon an application, therefore, protection mechanisms should be provided as tools for the enforcement of these varying policies.

5.10.3 Methods for Enforcement of Protection Mechanisms

As we know that a computer system is a collection of processes and objects (resources). Objects means hardware objects like CPU, memory, disk, printer, etc., and software objects like files, programs, semaphores, etc. Each object has a specific kind of operation applicable to it. For example, memory can be read or written, CPU can be only executed on, disk can be read and written, data files can be created, deleted, opened, read, written and closed. Thus, if these operations are known, a control mechanism can be implemented for each resource. A process should be allowed to access only those resources it has been authorized to access. A process should follow "Need-to-know" principle so that it should be able to access the resources, which it currently needs. This can be one way of implementing protection because only those resources, which are currently required, will need to be protected and others will be totally safe.

5.10.3.1 Access Rights

At any instance, protection should be provided to those resources, which may be currently used by a process. Thus, a domain known as protection domain can be defined for a process. Such a domain will contain the set of objects and the types of operations that can be invoked on each object. This means that domain is a set of <object, rights> pair. 'Rights' refer to the operations that can be invoked by a process on the corresponding object. These rights are also known as access rights of a particular process on the corresponding object for example, if a process is executing in domain D = <: data file F, (read, write) >; it can perform only read and write operations on the data file named 'F'.

The association of a process with a domain may be static or dynamic. The association can be static only when the set of resources available to a process is fixed throughout its lifetime. In case of static association, protection can be implemented by strictly adhering to the "need-to-know" principle. This implies that the domain should keep changing at different instances of a process' execution, as and when there is a change in the use of resources by this process. For example, consider a process P that needs read access (on a disk) in one phase and write access in another phase. Then in the first phase the domain should include only read access right on disk, i.e., <disk, read> and in the later phase, the domain should be modified to contain <disk, write>.

In case of dynamic association, a process can switch from one domain to another. Thus, here instead of changing the contents of a domain (to which a process may be statically associated as in case of static association), a new domain may be created with the changed content and the process may be switched to this new domain.

Examples of implementation of protection mechanisms using domain are:

i) **Dual mode** (Monitor – User mode) model of operating system execution is an example of protection mechanism because it ensures that if a process is in monitor mode, it can execute privileged instructions only and if it executes in user mode, it can invoke only non-privileged instructions. Memory protection can be implemented in multiprogramming environment where more than one user program may be executing in the user mode and may sometimes, interfere with each other.

ii) In UNIX, a domain is actually associated with a user. In this case, the sets of objects that can be accessed depend upon the identity of the user. Domain switching occurs when the user is changed – generally, this happens when one user logs out and another logs in or in a multiuser system when more than one user may be trying to access the same object. This can help in safe sharing of objects among different users. Therefore, the domain will contain <user-id, domain-bit>. This domain bit is also known as setuid bit. When a user (with user-id = A) starts executing a file (owned by user B), whose domain bit is off, the user-id of the process is set to A. This temporary user-id change ends when the process accessing the file exits or when the user logs off, which ever is earlier. When the domain bit is on, the user-id is not changed to A and remains B i.e. owner of the file. This implies that file is used by B and thus, should not be used by A.

5.10.3.2 Access Matrix

The access matrix model is the policy for user authentication and has several implementations such as access control lists

(ACLs) and capability lists. It is used to describe which users have access to what objects (resources). Thus, basically it checks the access rights of users on system resources. The access matrix model consists of four major parts:

i) A list of objects

ii) A list of subjects

iii) A function T that returns an object's type

iv) The matrix itself, with the objects (resources) making the columns and the subjects making the rows.

	Objects	
Subjects	Index.html	Java VM
John	r w x c	x
Doll	r c	—

Figure 5.12: Example Access Matrix

In the cells where a subject and object meet, lie the rights the subject has on that object. Some example access rights (as discussed in previous sub-section) are read, write, execute, list and delete. **Figure 1** shows an example access matrix.

An access matrix has several standard operations associated with it:

i) Entry of a right into a specified cell

ii) Removal of a right from a specified cell

iii) Creation of a subject

iv) Creation of an object

v) Removal of a subject

vi) Removal of an object

The access matrix shown in **figure 1** considers users as subjects and states that John can read, write, execute and copy the index.html file and that Doll can only read and copy this file. The subjects can also be processes and procedures. This implies that access matrix model can be used to define the access rights for processes also. It means that subjects are in fact the domains, which can be realized either as a user, or a process or a procedure. The generalized access matrix model is shown in **figure 2**.

Domain \ Object	File 1	File 2	Printer
D1	Read	Execute	Output
D2	——	Execute	——
D3	——	Read	Output

Figure 5.13: Generalized Access Matrix

Advantages of access matrix as a mechanism for implementing protection are:

It provides an appropriate mechanism for defining and implementing strict control for both the static and dynamic association between processes and domains. When a process is switched from one domain to another, an operation called switch is used. Thus, domain switching by processes can be controlled by including domains among the objects of the access matrix **figure 3** shows an access matrix with domains as objects.

This figure shows that a process executing in domain D1 can switch to domain D2. Similarly, a process executing in domain D2 can switch to domain D1 or domain D3.

It is thus an appropriate method of implementing protection mechanism.

Domain \ Object	File 1	File 2	File 3	D1	D2	D3	D4
D1	Read	—	Write	—	Switch	—	—
D2	—	Write	—	Switch	—	Switch	—
D3	Read	—	—	—	—	—	Switch
D4	—	Execute	—	Switch	—	—	—

Figure 5.14: Generalized Access Matrix with Domains as Objects

Disadvantages of this method are:

i) Although a useful model, access matrices are inefficient for storage of access rights in a computer system because they tend to be large and sparse,

ii) Mechanisms must be enforced to protect the access matrices themselves from change

Implementation of Access Matrices

The two most commonly used implementations arc access control lists (ACLs) and Capability lists.

1) **Access Control Lists (ACLs):** Access Control Lists (ACLs) are created by placing on each object a list of users and their rights to access that object. An example is already shown in **figure 1**, where the two objects index.html file and Java VM have a list of users (John and Doll) associated with them whose access rights have been written in the corresponding cells.

2) **Capability Lists:** Capability Lists are implemented by storing on each subject a list of rights the subject has for every object. This effectively gives each user, a sort of key ring. To remove access to a particular object, every user (subject) that has access to it must be "touched". A touch is an examination of a user's right to that object. **Figure 4** shows an example of implementation of the access matrix using capability lists.

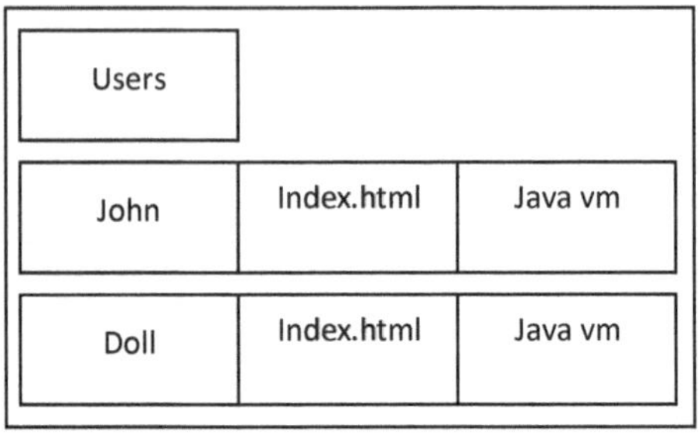

Figure 5.15: Implementation of the Access Matrix Using Capability Lists

Comparison of access lists and capabilities

Access Lists	Capabilities List
Each object (resource) has a list of pairs of the form <subject, access rights >	Each subject (user, process or procedure) has a list of pairs of the form <object, access rights>
It would be tedious to have separate listing for each subject (user), therefore, they are grouped into classes. For example, in UNIX, there are three classes: self, group, anybody else.	Here capabilities are the names of the objects. The objects not referred to in a capability list cannot be even named.
The default is: Everyone should be able to access a file.	The default is: No one should be able to access a file unless they have been given a capability.
Access lists are simple and are used in almost all file systems.	Capabilities are used in systems that need to be very secure as it prohibits sharing of information unless access is given to a subject.

5.11 Security and Its Goals

As discussed earlier, mechanisms are also needed to protect the external environment of a system.

Security violations (misuse) of the system can be either accidental or intentional. It is easier to protect against the accidental misuse than to protect against the intentional misuse. The intentional misuse can be of the following kinds:

i) Theft of information

ii) Unauthorized modification of data

iii) Unauthorized destruction of data

System can be protected from such threats at two levels:

i) **Physical:** The site containing the computer systems must be physically secured so that the intruders can be prohibited to enter the site.

ii) **Human:** Even the permitted users should be carefully screened so that the chance of authorizing a user who may give access to an intruder is reduced. It is obvious that if such a security system fails, the protection provided by the operating system will become almost useless.

Army databases, payroll databases and other such databases containing important financial data of an organization should be protected from intentional misuse. They are such sensitive data that remedy for the accidental loss should always be ready.

Even though such systems shall be kept under high security, there can be a chance of intruders coming in and trying to access the system. For this, the system hardware should also provide mechanisms to allow for the implementation of security features. Earlier operating systems like MS-DOS and Macintosh operating system did not provide much of the security as they were designed for the hardware, which did not provide memory or I/O protection. Recent operating systems such as Windows NT, Windows 2000 have been designed to provide the needed security features. Since this book deals with operating system concepts, we will discuss only the security measures that must be provided by the operating system. Further discussion of security at the human and physical levels is out of the scope of this test.

5.11.1 Authentication

Authentication of the user of a system is one of the major security issues associated with an operating system. It deals with authenticating a user who tries to log into the computer system rather than authenticating the user who tries to access a system resource. Generally, authentication of a user is based on:

i) User identifier and password (Passwords)

ii) Badge card possessed by a user (Artifacts)

iii) Finger prints, retina pattern or signature (Biometrics techniques). Let us discuss these techniques in detail.

Passwords

The password is the most common authentication mechanism based on sharing of a secret. In a password-based system each user has a password, which may initially be assigned by the system administrator. Many systems allow users to subsequently change their passwords. The system stores all user passwords and uses them to authenticate the users. When logging in, the system requests and the user supplies a presumably secret, user-specific password.

Passwords are popular because they require no special hardware and are relatively easy 10 implement. On the negative side, passwords offer limited protection, as they may be relatively easy to obtain or guess. Unencrypted passwords files stored in a system are obviously an easy prey. User-chosen passwords are frequently dictionary words or proper names. This makes them easy to remember and easy to guess. For example, user Ids, names or surnames, and their backward spellings typically account for a significant percentage of passwords.

System-chosen passwords, on the other hand, are usually random combinations of letters and numbers that are hard to guess but are also hard to remember. As a result, the users tend to write them down and store them in u handy place near the terminal. This can be easily located by someone and thus may no longer be a secret.

Various techniques have been proposed to strengthen the level of protection availed by the password mechanism. Unfortunately, most of these have drawbacks that reduce either their effectiveness or user acceptance. For example, password schemes may be multilevel, and users may be required to supply additional passwords at the system's request at random intervals during computer use. This tends to annoy the actual authorized users. Another technique is to have the system issue a dynamic challenge to the user after log-in. This challenge can be in the form of a random number generated by the computer, to which the user is supposed to apply a secret transformation, such as squaring and incrementing the value. Failure to do so may be used to detect unauthorized users.

Another technique, which attempts to discourage unauthorized users who attempt to log in by trying a series of different passwords, is to limit the number of consecutive attempts to log in the system. The number of consecutive log-in attempts may be controlled by disabling the user's account after a certain number of unsuccessful attempts. The user may subsequently reinstate the account by establishing his or her identity with the manager or a system administrator. The danger of this approach is the potential denial of service. This happens when a mischievous user disables the accounts of others by intentionally attempting to log in using other persons' ids, which are usually public. Such a user could easily knock out the whole system by disabling the accounts of all the administrators. To counteract this problem partly, some systems prohibit disabling when the number of active administrative accounts drops to one.

Artifact-Based Authentication

The artifacts commonly used for user authentication include machine-readable badges (usually with magnetic stripes) and electronic smart cards Badge or card readers may be installed in or near the terminals, and users are required to supply the artifact for authentication. In many systems, artifact identification is coupled with the use of a password. That is, the user must insert the card and then supply his or her password. This form of authentication is common with automated teller banking machines. The artifact-based systems work especially well in environments where the artifact is also used for other purposes.

For example, in some companies badges are required for employees to gain access to the organization's gate. The use of such a badge as an artifact for computer access and authentication can reduce the likelihood of the loss of an artifact. Smart cards can augment this scheme by keeping even the user's password within the card itself, which allows authentication without storage of passwords in the computer system. This makes it more difficult for mischievous users to uncover user passwords but the loss of such cards can be hazardous.

Biometrics Techniques

The third major group of authentication mechanisms is based on the unique characteristics of each user. Some user characteristics can be established by means of biometrics techniques. These fall into two basic categories:

i) Physiological characteristics, such as fingerprints, capillary patterns in the retina, hand geometry, and facial characteristics.

ii) Behavioral characteristics, such as signature dynamics, voice pattern, and timing of keystrokes.

In general, behavioral characteristics can vary with a user's state and thus may be susceptible to higher false acceptance or rejection rates. For example, signature dynamics and keystroke patterns may vary with a user's stress level and fatigue.

The biometrics detection devices are usually self-contained and independent of the computer system, which increases their resistance to common computer penetration methods and improves the potential for tamper proofing.

The primary advantages of biometrics authentication are the largely increased accuracy of user authentication and reduction of errors in security-conscious environments. For example, some retinal-scan devices claim an error rate as slow as 1 in 3 million (1 in trillion when both eyes are scanned).

The drawbacks of biometrics authentication include increased cost, potential invasion of privacy, and reluctance of some users.

5.11.2 Encryption

As computer networks gain popularity, more sensitive information is being transmitted over channels where eavesdropping and message interception is possible. Thus, the operating system should have some provision to fight such situations i.e. to protect the data that are transferred over the network.

Encryption is one such mechanism, which allows such data to be scrambled so that even if some one intercepts it on the network, it is not readable to him/her. Thus, the basic purpose of encryption is to make the data transfer secure over the network.

Encryption works as:

i) It transforms information from ("Clear" or "plain text") to coded information ("Cipher text"), which cannot be read by outside parties.

ii) This transformation process is controlled by an algorithm and a key.

iii) This process should be reversible so that the intended recipient can read the information transmitted to him in the form of cipher text. But for this a decryption mechanism which decrypts (decodes) the cipher text to plain text is must. Figure 12.5 shows a general encryption and decryption mechanism.

The main challenge in using this approach is the development of encryption schemes that are impossible to break.

These are two kinds of encryption:

i) 'Symmetrical Encryption' or secret key which uses a single key to encrypt and decrypt the transmitted data.

ii) 'Asymmetrical Encryption' which uses 'Private Key', in which one key is used to encrypt and another to decrypt the transmitted data.

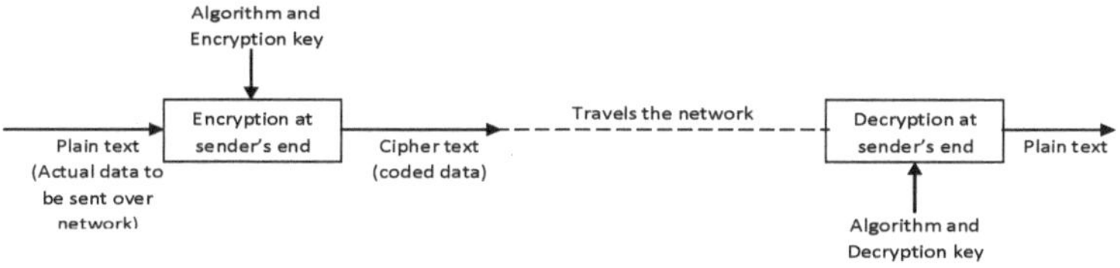

Figure 5.16: General Encryption and Decryption

Encryption Schemes

i) One scheme (that uses single secret key) called Data Encryption Standard (DES), was once adopted as standard for encryption. This scheme, however, suffers from key-distribution problem. Before communication can take place, the secret keys must be sent securely to both the sender and the receiver. This task itself is prone to the threat of eves dropping by the unauthorized users who may be trying hard to know the secret keys.

ii) A solution to the problem encountered in DES is to use a .scheme known as public-key-encryption scheme. In this scheme, each user has both a public and a private key, and two users can communicate knowing only each other's public key. The algorithms based on this concept are believed to be almost unbreakable and therefore, this scheme is the most preferred and reliable scheme, for secure network communication.

5.11.3 Viruses, Worms and Trojans

Let us first try to find out what is a Virus, a Worm and a Trojan?

A computer virus is a small program written to alter the way a computer operates and it executes without the permission or knowledge of the user. A program is a virus if it meets the two criteria:

i) It must execute itself.

ii) It must replicate itself, for example, it may replace other executable files with a copy of the virus infected file. File infector viruses, boot sector viruses, master boot record viruses, multi-partite viruses and macro viruses are few kind of known viruses and this classification depends upon their target area or mode of operation.

Worms are basically the programs that replicate themselves from system to system without the use of a host file. They contain malicious code that can cause major damage to the files, software and data on a computer. The most insidious characteristic of a worm is its ability to distribute functional copies of itself to other computer systems. While viruses rely on attaching to another program to be executed, worms are free agents that can roam independently through networks and thus propagate and wreak havoc.

There are several ways that worms can get into a computer. The most common is through the Internet and E-mail. PrettyPark.worm is a prevalent example.

Trojan horses are impostors - files that claim to be something desirable, but in fact, are malicious. A very important distinction from true viruses is that they do not replicate themselves, as viruses do. Trojans contain malicious code, that, when triggered, cause loss, or even theft, of data. In order for a Trojan horse to spread, the user must invite these programs onto his computer - for example, by opening an e-mail attachment. The PWSteal. Trojan is a Trojan.

Dealing with Viruses

The existence of a computer virus typically encompasses four stages:

i) Dormancy

ii) Propagation

iii) Triggering

iv) Damage

Upon infecting a new machine or a new program, the computer virus may remain dormant for a while so that its presence is not suspected. Computer viruses are commonly spread through acquisition of programs directly or indirectly obtained from computer networks and bulletin boards in the form of shareware or public domain programs. Unlike worms, viruses need not propagate themselves via networks but may be spread by program sharing between users, A machine becomes infected by executing a contaminated program. However, networks can accelerate spreading of viruses, especially when shared programs residing in the server become contaminated.

The duration of the dormant period may vary depending on the type of mechanism being used. The virus may wait a certain number of executions of the host program or the elapsing of a certain period of time before progressing to the next stage - propagation, in the propagation stage, the virus attempts to infect other programs on the host machine. The target can also be the operating system and the boot block. For example, a floppy disk may be contaminated just by having its directory listed on the infected machine

In order for the virus to spread, the infected carrier program must be executed. The virus spreads by searching the system, typically the disk, for uninfected programs and attaching itself to them. Although propagation of viruses is possible in any programmable computer, it is easier in personal computers with unprotected operating systems. Depending on the particular mechanism in use, the code of virus modifies an executable file in such a manner that it receives control upon program activation. When the infected program is executed, the virus code receives control, and performs the work appropriate for the stage that it is in. Control is then usually returned to the host program for normal operations. In this way, the virus can hide its existence all the way through the triggering stage.

After completing the self-propagation stage, the trigger is activated to facilitate transition to the damage stage. The trigger may be defined as a count of replications, or it can be timer-based so as to cause the damage at some specific time or date, such as September the 15th. The damage itself can range from printing a message announcing the presence of the virus, to malignant damage such as erasure of files or damaging of the boot block.

Major safeguards against viruses are:

There is no known general vaccine for computer viruses. As usual, prevention is the best protection. Common preventive measures include careful screening of all newly acquired software, frequent backups and a combination of utilities such as integrity checkers, monitoring programs and virus removers.

i) **Integrity checkers:** These are programs that attempt to detect modifications of other programs by calculating their checksums. They are should be run quite frequently, such as upon each boot. Since virus infection modifies the size of the affected program, the integrity checker can detect and report such changes.

ii) **Monitoring programs:** Monitoring programs are permanent resident (daemon) programs that continuously check certain memory and I/O operations for suspicious behavior that may be attributable to viruses. Monitoring programs are effectively an extension of operating system that tries to plug the security holes known or likely to be exploited by viruses.

iii) **Virus removers:** These are programs that scan system storage for signatures and patterns that belong to viruses known to the program author. They can detect and remove known viruses even in the dormant stage (the very first stage when a virus infects a machine or a new program) However, virus removers cannot cope with unknown viruses. Virus-remover programs need to be updated frequently in order to keep up with new types of viruses.

iv) **Purchasing unopened software:** Purchasing unopened software from vendors, avoiding free or pirated copies from public sources, avoiding floppy-disk exchange are the safest ways of preventing virus infection.

Dealing with Worms

Computer-worm programs usually do not cause any direct damage to the other programs and files in a computer system that they invade. However, they tend to consume large amounts of resources for their own dissemination, thus denying service to users. A computer worm typically operates by sending copies of itself to other machines in a network. The usual line of attack is the users' mailing lists, which contain the names and addresses of other reachable machines. After gaining access to a mailing list, the worm sends copies of itself (an executable program) to some or all listed machines Depending on its sophistication, upon arrival at a new destination, the worm may or may not check whether the new destination is already infected. If it is not infected or if no check is made, the worm will attempt to gain access to the local mailing lists for further spreading. As a result, computers on the network and the network itself become flooded with copies of executing and traveling worms. This infection usually spreads quickly and drowns the entire system by consuming processing time and network bandwidth so that only little or none of the any other works and communication can proceed.

Two major safeguards against computer worms are:

i) **Making penetration of each machine difficult:** Penetration attempts may be averted by strengthening system security, especially in the areas of mailing utilities, passwords, and access control to the mailing lists.

ii) **Hindering worm spreading:** Spreading of executable programs may be curtailed by means of checkpoints in the communication system. For example, the network interface can prohibit transfers of executable programs and command files, or require explicit operator or user intervention as a condition for each particular acceptance.

5.11.4 Threat Monitoring

The security of a system can be improved by some management techniques. One such technique is Threat-monitoring. Threat monitoring implies that the system can check for suspicious patterns of activity in an attempt to detect a security violation.

The techniques that can be used for threat monitoring are:

i) A time sharing system can keep the count of the number of incorrect passwords given, when a user is trying to log in. More than a few incorrect attempts may signal an attempt to guess a password.

ii) Audit log is another common technique used for threat monitoring. An audit log records the time of use, the details of users, and types of all the accesses to an object. After the security has been violated, the audit log can be used to determine how and when the problem occurred and perhaps what amount of damage was done. This information can be useful for recovery from security violation as well as in the development of tighter security measures to prevent future problems.

iii) The system can be scanned periodically for security holes. Scanning can be done when the system has less traffic.

Such a scan can check a variety of aspects of the system. It can check for unexpectedly long running processes, existence of Trojans or some unauthorized programs in system directories, improper protection on system data files, such as the password file, device drivers, or even the operating system kernel itself.

The problems encountered in the security scan can either be fixed automatically or reported to the system manager.

iv) As the use of Internee is becoming very popular and as it is becoming an indispensable resource for many computers and individuals, protection from viruses and worms (that might invade the computer system through the Internet) is a very essential aspect of security. One solution to this problem is the use of a firewall. A firewall is basically a program (i.e. a software) or a hardware device that filters the information coming through the Internet connection into the company's private network or the individual user's system. **Figure 6** shows how can a firewall be used. There are many ways that miscreant people may use to access or abuse unprotected computers. These include using remote login to control a remote computer and run some hazardous program on it. Other threats involve sending of spams (junk mails), hijacking of SMTP (Simple Mail Transfer Protocol) session and gaining access to a list of e-mail addresses, which can be used to send spams to thousands of users. All above stated threats and many more related to the unsecured use of Internet can be stopped by firewall. The entire network traffic can be restricted to travel through the firewall so that only certain types of information such as e-mail can get through. Spams cannot be filtered until the firewall stops an e-mail to get through which is not possible in today's world where almost everyone is using e-mail. It also stops anyone on the outside, from remotely logging into a computer in a private network of an organization.

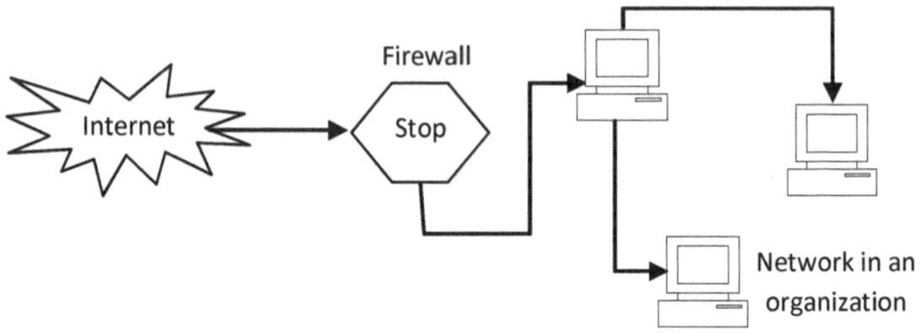

Figure 5.17: Network Security through Firewall

PRACTICE QUESTIONS

Subjective Questions:

Q.1. How access matrix is useful in enforcement of file system protection and security?

Q.2. Write short notes on followings:

- Redundant Array of Inexpensive Disks
- Boot block

Q.3. What is Directory? Define any two ways to implement the directory.

Q.4. Consider the situation in which the disk read/write head is currently located at track 45 (of tracks 0-255) and moving in the positive direction. Assume that the following track requests have been made in this order: 40, 67, 11, 240, 87. What is the order in which C-SCAN and LOOK would service these requests and what is the total seek distance?

Q.5. Suppose track request are 95, 180, 34, 119, 11, 123, 62, 64 with the Read-write head initially at the track 50. If there are 200 tracks numbered from 0 to 199, find the total head movements using SCAN and SSTF approach.

Q.6. Why the bitmap for file allocation must be kept on mass storage, rather than in main memory?

Q.7. Explain the following types of buffering:

- Double Buffering
- Circular Buffering

Q.8. Explain the different Disk performance Parameters.

Q.9. Give the discussion about file accessing methods.

Q.10. Explain the following file system organization:

- Linked List Allocation Using an Index
- l-nodes

Q.11. Discuss the reasons why the operating system might require accurate information on how blocks are stored on a disk. How could the operating system improve file system performance with this knowledge?

Q.12. Could a RAID Level 1 organization achieve better performance for read requests than a RAID Level 0 organization (with non-redundant striping of data)? If so, how?

Q.13. Compare the goals of disk scheduling with those of CPU scheduling. What are the similarities? What are the differences?

Q.14. Consider the following scenario

- Work Queue: 23, 89, 132, 42, 187
- There are 200 cylinders numbered from 0 - 199
- The disk head stars at number 100

Find the total head movement for servicing all request using Look and C-Scan Algorithm.

Q.15. A process uses several buffers while processing a file containing block records. If a system failure occurs during its execution, is it possible to resume execution of the process from the point of failure.

Supplementary Questions:

Q.1. Consider a file system on a disk that has both logical and physical block size of 512 bytes. Assume the information about each file is already in the memory. For each of the three allocation strategies (contiguous and indexed), answer following questions:

- How is the logical to physical address mapping accomplished in this system? (For indexed allocation, assume that a file is always less than 512 blocks long)
- If we are currently at logical block 10 and want to access logical block 4 how many physical blocks must be read from the disk?

Q.2. Describe an encryption method provided in Unix to secure files. How does one retrieve an encrypted file using an encryption command? Explain the basic principle.

Short Answer Type Questions:

Q.1. What is seek time?

Q.2. What is the problem with SCAN scheduling with disks in brief?

Q.3. Enlist the different levels of RAID.

Q.4. Define parity.

Q.5. Provide examples of at least three program threats.

Q.6. What are the advantages of linked list allocation of files?

Q.7. How raid is configured in OS level?

Q.8. What are the two fundamental ways of accessing a file?

Q.9. Define the term cylinder in contest with hard disk.

Q.10. What Is Check Consistency?

■■■

Made in United States
Troutdale, OR
11/03/2026

56847559R00126